GW00372917

COLLECTING
PENS

by Edward Kiersh

HOUSE OF COLLECTIBLES

NEW YORK   TORONTO   LONDON   SYDNEY   AUCKLAND

House of Collectibles and colophon are registered trademarks of Random House, Inc.

RANDOM HOUSE is a registered trademark of Random House, Inc.

This book is available for special discounts for bulk purchases for sales promotions or premiums. Special editions, including personalized covers, excerpts of existing books, and corporate imprints, can be created in large quantities for special needs. For more information, write to Special Markets/Premium Sales, 1745 Broadway, MD 6-2, New York, NY, 10019 or e-mail *specialmarkets@randomhouse.com*.

Please address inquiries about electronic licensing of any products for use on a network, in software, or on CD-ROM to the Subsidiary Rights Department, Random House Information Group, fax 212-572-6003.

Visit the House of Collectibles Web site:
www.houseofcollectibles.com

Library of Congress Cataloging-in-Publication Data is available.

Printed in the United States of America

10 9 8 7 6 5 4 3 2 1

ISBN-10: 0-375-72069-3
ISBN-13: 978-0-375-72069-7

CONTENTS

Writing a book involves more than research.
It also demands the patience
and support of family members.

This book is dedicated to my wife, Nancy,
and son, Aaron, for having faith in me.

ACKNOWLEDGMENTS

My hope was to write a book that emphasized the joys of pen collecting, and in that undertaking I was helped generously by many people.

My encouraging and always enthusiastic Random House editor, Oriana Leckert, worked tirelessly on this project, and had faith in it throughout. She saw the potential in this book, and for that I'll always be grateful.

Numerous pen experts also provided tremendous assistance. Pen lover and photographer Jim Mamoulides, along with furnishing wonderful photos, could always be depended upon for wise observations and suggestions. Various web sites, and true pen aficionados such as David Nishimura, Geoffrey Berliner, Richard C. "Rick" Conner, Roger Cromwell, Terry Wiederlight, the folks at GoPens, Jim Gaston, Jim Griffiths, and Max of 1001Pens, were similarly important to the writing of this book.

Finally, I'd like to thank the editors of *Cigar Aficionado* and the *Robb Report,* who led me to recognize the beauty of collectible pens years ago, and gave me the opportunity to write about these wonderful writing instruments. Then there's my agent, Scott A. Travers. He was a friend in this endeavor and, so, a hearty thanks.

INTRODUCTION: THE FINE POINTS

The pen has always been mightier than the sword. But now, as enthusiasts discover the handcrafted genius and precision of these writing instruments, the relatively uncharted universe of pen collecting is generating more excitement than ever.

From **Parker Snakes** and **Waterman Patricians** to **Montblanc Hemingways** and the many sleeper brands with terrific upside potential, vintage fountain pens are selling for record prices at auctions. These hand-painted, delicately lacquered works of art were once dismissed as mere throwaway items at garage sales and flea markets. Few people had any idea that messy, smudge-prone fountain pens with durable, impact-resistant barrels containing reservoirs of ink and feed mechanisms that relied on gravity or surface tension to supply the ink to a nib would become statement-making, recession-proof assets.

But ever since Christie's conducted the first "classic pen" auction in 1976, giving the market instant legitimacy, vintage pieces have taken on an aura or cachet approaching that of prized works of art. A *maki-e* lacquered 1928–30 **Namiki Giant**, embellished with two dragons poised against a backdrop of lightning bolts and gold storm clouds, recently sold for $290,000. Another Namiki decorated with gold powder flecks and intricate detailing of a dragon hovering amid silver and red storm clouds went for $180,000, and a 1905 **Parker Aztec** with an ornamental Awanyu Indian chief head typically sells for $50,000 to $110,000.

What is feeding this fervor? Vintage fountain pens, particularly those rare pieces with precious metals or jewels, inlaid mother-of-pearl stones, and historical cachet, epitomize the new passion for "retro" craftsmanship. Collectors, whether they collect mechanical watches, antique cameras, or pens, are taking a renewed interest in meticulously detailed items from America's past. An interestingly designed pen, in contrast to a mass-produced Bic, conveys a dramatic sense of style and discernment; and best of all, amassing a respectable collection of pens is relatively affordable. There are indisputable bargains that can still be discovered, and searching for a rare, historical, or beautiful pen is often a fun-filled adventure. The availability of prized items has made pens even more alluring. This flourishing "pen renaissance" is so strong that the enthusiasm has spawned hundreds of Internet sites, dozens of clubs, several magazines, a flood of limited editions, and a constant schedule of shows where thousands of vintage pens can be touched, admired, and sampled to determine if they meet an individual's personal requirements.

Much of this collecting frenzy is also caused by a burgeoning backlash against the anonymity and sterility of cyberspace. In a world dominated by the dulling sameness of electronic printouts, pens (along with old-fashioned bottles of ink) provide an intimate, highly personalized interaction with writing. Far more personally revealing than any fax or e-mail, the slants and strokes of a handwritten note demand a slowing down, an attention to detail that's achieved only with the mind and hand working beautifully together.

Such a high touch enterprise, which relies on an iridium-tipped gold nib individually suited to a person's unique writing style, is enlivened by many individualistic flourishes. Famous entertainer and avid pen collector Bill Cosby has said, "Writing by hand is an art form. It's an excitement, a personalized expression which lets you see your mind's blood unfold on paper."

A man of relatively simple tastes who's amassed quite a number of Bics and ballpoints, Cosby prefers pens without "a Tiffany array of diamonds and rubies." Other collectors, thrilled by the chase of discovering a rare treasure with *repoussé* ornamentation, are increasingly spending large sums on pens that are exquisitely lacquered (like many of Namiki's masterworks) and sheathed with gold or silver overlays.

Whatever your pleasure (or checking account balance), pen collecting is fun, and potentially profitable. A few choices must be made, of course. New collectors will have to wrestle with the age-old dilemma pitting vintage pieces such as uniquely styled Parkers and Watermans against equally attractive contemporary pens from the 1960s and modern limited editions. Does a new collector buy pens that must be restored? Or is it wise to acquire only pens that show no traces of discoloration, warping, worn or missing parts, or chips, and need no mechanical repairs?

Pen collecting is still a blossoming hobby, and although entering this new world can lead to a few mistakes (there is no clear-cut or standardized grading system for pens, for example), exploring such territory can also be thrilling. At the outset it might be wise to purchase only relatively inexpensive pens, pieces that are a no-risk way to discover if collecting pens suits your aesthetic and acquisitive fancy. Later the real fun begins. Enthusiasts will have a variety of choices among five- and six-figure trophy pieces from the 1920s and '30s, and stunning contemporary limited editions from companies such as Omas, Delta, Aurora, and Montblanc.

No matter what collecting strategy you choose, hobbyists must know their pen basics. Talk with experts. Go to pen shows. Learn the language of collecting. This guide will help you in that world, and will also provide an overview of which pens are smart investments and why, and tips from various experts on how to avoid the market's pitfalls. Along with a comprehensive price list, this book offers practical advice that will surely help you find the write stuff.

1

THE MYSTIQUE OF THE FOUNTAIN PEN: WHAT TO COLLECT AND HOW

Now that inexpensive, mass-produced, and low-maintenance ballpoints are easily available, the rationale for using a fine fountain pen is less obvious than it was in the early to mid-1900s. At that time, a uniquely designed, highly finished pen with a 14k gold nib was a necessity, a workaday tool (there were no ballpoint pens until 1938); whereas today, handcrafted writing instruments play a more intriguing role as statements of art and symbols of personal taste and sophistication.

But as well as being fun, providing an impetus to write more finely composed letters, and offering a discriminating way to slow down or escape the mad rush of modern life, fountain pens are a wise, transportable, liquid investment. Highly coveted as arti-

Detail of Waterman #32 Nib and Imprint 1920s

Mabie Todd Swan Hand Engraved 14 Karat Gold Eyedropper Pen circa 1912

facts from an era when craftsmanship was far less mechanized and far more labor-intensive, many vintage pieces are attracting unprecedented prices at auctions and at pen shows. Newly issued limited editions are showing equal strength, particularly the recently introduced $12,500 **Parker Snake**, which sold for 50 percent over list price soon after it was released. And then there's the case of the infamous **Montblanc Alexandre Dumas** three-piece sets. In 1966, Montblanc released a three-piece set—which included a fountain pen, a ballpoint pen, and a pencil—celebrating the life and work of the famous French author of *The Three Musketeers* and *The Count of Monte Cristo*, with his signature on the pen. Montblanc released the first 1,800 sets with the

Pen Repair in Progress

Conway Stewart 479—Note Chased Cap and Barrel

wrong signature, or, more precisely, the signature of Dumas's illegitimate son, an author who also was named Alexandre Dumas. Before this mistake was noticed by the company, sharp-eyed collectors snatched up all the sets, which quickly rose 300 percent in value.

Though such mistakes are rare, the *Affaire Dumas* dramatizes an essential aspect of pen buying that all new collectors should appreciate: With the details and craftsmanship that go into the production of pens—especially the more expensive ones—you would do well to fully study a pen, look at its design elements, and determine whether it is so aesthetically or functionally appealing that it "sings" to you.

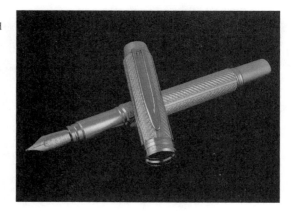

Waterman Etoile Limited Edition 1993

Sheaffer Triumph Sentinel circa 1947, a Celluloid Pen

Once a pen passes this personal test, there are other factors to consider. Rarity, the pen's pedigree or the prestige it commands in the marketplace, its technical design, aesthetics, and certainly the pen's condition, the presence of any supporting documentation such as manuals, other papers, and original box—these are all important elements that can affect the value and appeal of a pen. Well-informed collectors realize that pens from reputable companies and unique, high-quality pieces that significantly affected pen-making history are the blue chips—the items that stand the best chance of rising in value every year.

As New York's Fountain Pen Hospital's Terry Wieder-light says, "Buyers must be selective. Unlike a few years ago, not every limited [edition] is going to rise

25 percent. The savvy consumer can still enjoy a terrific hobby and profit. But the investment trick is to only buy pens with unquestioned craftsmanship from companies with proven track records. Do your homework. Then go for the best, the manufacturers with real history."

That learning process begins at pen shows that are regularly held in most major U.S. cities, and by actually using nibs, filling systems, casing materials, and other refinements. Prospective collectors should also talk to other enthusiasts at these shows and determine which dealers are the most reputable.

Common lower-priced items can be bought without much worry. But once novices enter the nerve-rattling world of auctions and pursue investment-quality blue chips, they must know much more than their introductory ABCs. In the higher-priced categories, which are dominated by Watermans, Parkers, and other golden-age pens, subtle distinctions in color, construction, and ornamentation markedly affect values. A collector must have a trained eye to discern those differences, and such risk-reducing expertise comes only by doing more homework.

"Read books, learn what pens sold for at auctions, go to shows, talk with other collectors, and above all develop your tastes and determine what's available that you actually like," advises Geoffrey Berliner, a collector and owner of Berliner Pen, a vintage pen shop in New York City. "There are no hard and fast rules here, as beginners could specialize in pens from a certain time period, like art deco or the machine age. It's just a mistake to take some so-called expert's advice and to buy only early Parkers. This has burned people, and I really believe if collectors genuinely like something, they'll be more successful," Berliner says.

Dismissing the "Parker Strategy" as just too expensive, Berliner insists the "sleeper" approach is potentially more rewarding. "It's like discounted stocks: you look for the ones that people don't know much about and which have great earning potential. While anyone can buy just Parkers and Watermans, you separate the wisest buyers when they go for the sleepers—

Conklin
Black and
Cream
circa 1928

Sheaffer
Balance
Ebonized
Pearl circa
1937

unknown pens like A. A. Waterman, Aiken Lambert, and John Holland. These are very high quality and can be bought at a good price. They don't have cachet value now, but very easily could in the future."

Risks still abound. A pen can be a hot buy for a certain time period, yet once word spreads that it's in abundant supply, prices can plummet virtually overnight. Rarities such as mother-of-pearl **Pregnant Parkers**, which are worth about $9,000 or **Parker Swastikas,** worth about $30,000, can be viewed as perennial blue chips, always appreciating in value. (The swastika, also known as a Navajo cross, is an ancient good-luck symbol dating back some 3,000 years. The word comes from the Sanskrit *svasti*, well-being.) But as dramatized by **Ever-**

sharp Dorics, which recently became very popular, only to quickly slump, pens go in and out of favor. Investors have to be prepared for those wild swings and realize that although quick profits are possible, the better bet is holding items for the long term.

A go-slow approach has another benefit. It helps shield buyers from unscrupulous dealers and other sellers. There are all sorts of scams to watch out for, and one of the most common is counterfeiting—silver and metal overlays can be used to hide defects, or, as David Nishimura, a vintage pen aficionado, warns, be "taken from other pens of less prestigious brands." See his excellent web site *www.vintagepens.com* for more tips about "enhanced" pens, fakes, and forgeries.

"Beginners shouldn't go out and immediately spend a lot of money," Berliner advises. "Anyone with an untrained eye won't be able to tell when parts have been replaced, if a clip is a reproduction. Acetones can be used to minimize burn holes or cracks. New buyers simply can't spot counterfeit parts, and when selling these 'restored' pens, they take a bath."

A Brief Glossary of Pen Terms

To artfully—and profitably—collect choice pens of every description, the new enthusiast must visit trade shows, auctions, and dealers' shops and network with fellow aficionados. This world will be seductive, studded with well-crafted rarities. But to truly appreciate these delights, the savvy buyer has to think and talk like an expert. Understanding and using the following terms will add to your enjoyment of collecting, make you feel at home among seasoned collectors, and just might help you discover a few beauties. What follows is a short, introductory list of terms. For a complete list of pen terminology, please see the Glossary at the back of the book.

- **Band** A decorative metal ring that encircles the cap and helps prevent the cap from cracking.
- **Barrel** The main body of the fountain pen. Whether round, stubby-shaped, or thin, this plastic, celluloid, or hard rubber piece holds the nib, feed, ink, and filling mechanism.

- **Cap** A protective and removable cover, preventing damage to the nib, this piece can be a slip-on or can be threaded or screwed onto the pen.
- **Clip** The metal or plastic clasp that allows a pen to be attached to a pocket.
- **Cracks** Typically found in older hard rubber and plastic pens, these flaws predictably lower a vintage piece's value.
- **Feed** Located under the nib, this part can best be compared to a canal or strait through which the ink flows from its reservoir to the nib.
- **Filling Mechanism** Though there are a variety of fillers among fountain pens, drawing ink into a rubber sac or some other feature inside the barrel typically involves the expelling of air and the pulling of ink into a chamber.
- **Limited Edition** Pens produced in small, numbered quantities. Usually rarer and more valuable than mass-produced pens.
- **Nib** The metal, steel, gold-plated, or gold point from which the ink flows to give fountain pen writing its distinctive style. There are italic nibs, stub nibs, two-tone nibs, and warranted nibs; and at the tip of many nibs is an iridium metal ball to reduce wear.
- **Sac** The cylindrical ink reservoir inside the barrel, traditionally made of rubber or latex. A metal pressure bar presses against this sac to create a vacuum and fill the pen.
- **Section** The tubular piece or grip (where the pen is usually held) where the nib and feed are located.
- **Vintage** This term is inexact. Some experts think it describes the highly sought-after, highly priced, and distinctively designed pens that were produced from the late nineteenth century to the 1930s. Other aficionados maintain the vintage tag should apply even to those mass-produced pens that were offered up to the 1960s.

Careful First Steps

How does the new collector avoid pitfalls? This section will help you learn just that.

First, go to pen shows and network with other collectors. Talk to them about dealers and try to determine who can be trusted. Patronize only those dealers—or Internet sites—that offer full disclosure and money-back guarantees.

As a beginner, first buy inexpensive pens. More costly pieces should be purchased only after this hobby proves to be of definite interest and excitement, and when you have familiarized yourself with the field. Purchasing a few expensive, high-quality pens is often a wiser strategy than acquiring many lesser-priced items, or those of questionable quality.

"Buy the best you can," advises longtime collector and retailer Roger Cromwell, who is known for his expert repairing of pens and for his web site, *Penopoly.com* (not to be confused with Rick Conner's site, *www.rick conner.net/penoply*, without the second o). "Just don't buy a handful of pens. Buy quality pens, for these are the ones that stand the best chance of rising in value. So rather than buy indiscriminately, or several pens at any one time, be selective, and buy that one special pen. Later on you can trade that one really good piece for several pens that can be used to diversify a collection, or that can actually be used, or one that can be traded for another high-quality piece."

An important thing to remember when looking at pens, as with most collectibles, is condition, condition, condition. This is key to investment potential and also to enjoying acquisitions. Inspect pens thoroughly before buying, and avoid badly worn pens. Always try out a pen, write with it, and see if it suits your handwriting style. When attending flea markets and pen shows, choose pens that feel comfortable in your hand. Make sure the ink flows smoothly. As Geoffrey Berliner suggests, nibs should glide over the paper, not scratch against it. Technical mastery, exquisite design, and historical importance are also critical in appraising values. But good-looking pens are just good-looking keepsakes if they don't write well. If a pen doesn't perform, it's worthless. A famous adage in the pen world is, "It's the nib that makes the pen, not the pen that makes the nib."

When inspecting pens, use a magnifier and a good light source. Make sure that pens are straight. Check for hairline cracks with the magnifier. Look for mechanical damage. See if the cap and barrel are properly aligned. Are there any missing parts? Are there any missing manufacturer's imprints? Is the pen discolored or stained? Loose cap bands are a danger sign. Excessively polished pens, especially if the original markings have been obliterated, are also highly questionable.

Go to auctions to learn about the market and price valuations. During the learning process don't buy anything. Take your time. Eventually, set a budget and stick to your limits. Always remember that many auctions are dumping grounds for flawed or restored items, although they can also be a rich source for high-end pieces.

If possible, speak to more experienced collectors about the pens that are being auctioned. It's also vital to remember that all sales are final. When buying expensive pens at auctions, or anywhere else, make sure to get professional advice until you are more sure of yourself.

Far more appealing than pen shows, antiques auctions are a place where pen specialists are not as likely to dominate the proceedings. In many instances, pens are overlooked at these furniture and art sales, because the people in attendance often know very little about pens. That can translate into bargain prices for the sharp-eyed beginner.

Surf the Internet to learn about historical perspectives, buying trends, and pen prices. But be cautious in cyberspace; anonymity conceals many crimes. To buy on the Internet, the aspiring collector must be very good, and very educated. All too often a person selling a pen on a site such as eBay has an unrealistic estimation of what a mint or near mint pen is. Too often these overrated pens have flaws. A better strategy when first building a collection is to really savor the joy of buying a pen by touching it, seeing how it performs, and enjoying that special moment when the pen is first acquired.

Limited edition pens can be smart investments, but they pose their own risks, especially now that scores of companies are issuing highly ornamented items. Here, too, buyers must be extremely selective, because the overproduced supply of commemoratives has lowered the value of many new releases. When buying limited editions, think in the long term and select those pens with a historical concept or dimension, instead of faddish pieces. Penopoly's Roger Cromwell warns, "If you're going to invest in a fountain pen, make sure it's a vintage piece. New pens can cost you five, ten, or fifteen thousand dollars, but the minute it's bought, the value plummets, maybe even in half. There's a $14,000 pen out there that can't even be sold for $3,000. People must be very careful when buying new. If you're going to buy new, this is a very long-term investment, in many cases a fifty-year investment. You must insist on very low production if you're buying new. The better bet is to buy a vintage pen that has a proven track record."

Above all, buy pens to have fun, not just to make a profit. As with all collectibles, pens go up and down in value. The one constant is enjoying the hobby, along with the thrill of the chase. As Cromwell advises, "It's always the greatest fun to find a pen on your own. That's why I tell people to attend pen shows. This is where the best deals are. People are there unloading their inventory. Dealers must discount their pens at these shows since there are so many competitors at these gatherings. If a pen is rare, there's a good chance the collector will find it at one of these shows. Plus, because of all the people selling pens, buyers have a lot more leverage at these shows, and that, too, translates into fun."

Preserving the Pen Maker's Art
Wonderfully rich in color, hand-carved with numerous elegant refinements, and masterpieces of engineering, fountain pens are luxurious and functional accessories. They are celebratory trophies, lovely objets d'art,

in many cases direct descendants of gold- or silver-smithing traditions, not to mention durable writing instruments.

Adorned with specially cut nibs, intricately crafted filling mechanisms, *maki-e* lacquered, *guilloche*, or *repoussé* patterns, pens are also delicate gems. Prone to scratching, discoloration over time, the corrosive effects of ink, ossification of rubber sacs, clogging, and the inevitable cracking of plastics, these mechanical instruments must be treated with delicacy and kindness. Pens and their parts are built to last, but to guarantee years of smooth writing, and to protect their enchanting appearance, certain do's and don'ts must be followed, which will be covered throughout this book.

Ink: The Beauty and the Beast

Despite their vivid colors and artistic appeal, not all inks are created equal. Some are to be relished, whereas others should be avoided because they discolor barrels and caps and can clog the feed assembly. These culprits usually contain too much dye and are made with finely ground pigments that block the capillary action of a pen, preventing a smooth flow through the internal channels. Avoid highly saturated inks, which are notorious for discoloring pens. India inks are designed for dip pens and will clog fountain pens. India inks should not be used in fountain pens unless the pen manufacturer specifically states that it is safe. Use fresh ink, not ink that has been lying around for months. David Nishimura recommends using Parker's **Quink**, Sheaffer's **Skrip**, and Pelikan's **4001**.

No matter what ink you use, remember that it's still a fluid, prone to evaporation, and that these escaping dyes can clog a pen. Ink also dries out and gets encrusted when exposed to air under the nib or in the ink-supply channel. When this happens, the built-up residue is similar to plaque in the heart's arteries: nothing flows. Everything becomes clogged. As noted by pen dealers and experts such as Richard Binder, Geoffrey Berliner, and David Nishimura, there are many ways to avoid this problem.

- Keep a pen filled with a full supply of ink—but empty it before taking it on an airplane.
- When carrying pens, Nishimura advises, "Carry your pen nib upwards, and you should have no trouble with leakage. Keep your pen full of ink, since ink flow can become irregular if the ink chamber is close to empty. Ninety-five percent of leaky pens can be cured by the above two precautions."
- Use bonded or acid-free papers.
- If a pen isn't going to be used for an extended period of time, don't leave ink in it. A pen with ink in it shouldn't lie idle for more than a week.
- Store pens upright, with the nib pointed upward.

Pens, especially those that are used repeatedly, should be thoroughly drained every month or so. To flush a pen of any remaining ink or sediments, use cool or luke-warm water (preferably distilled), and be persistent. Flush the pen several times. But other than the nib assembly, don't immerse a pen into water. As Nishimura warns, "Pens are designed to hold liquids, not to be immersed in them. If the ink gets into the inside of the cap, wipe it out with a damp cotton swab. Dunking the entire cap (or the entire barrel) is unnecessary, and may harm your pen. If your pen is clogged with dried ink, soak it by placing it nib-down in only enough water to cover the nib and the lower part of the section, leaving the barrel dry." To fully clean a pen, shake it repeatedly, the way you would shake a thermometer.

Heat and light can have a deleterious effect on pens. If you want to preserve the pens' original color, don't store them in direct sunlight. Pen boxes, leather cases, and cabinets are safe places to keep pens. They shouldn't be kept in tins and plastic bags, or any other containers with chemical agents that could destroy the pens' luster and natural colors.

Nibs: The Pen's Unique Personality

They come in various shapes, such as round, stub, or italic. Some are malleable, whereas others are rigid and offer little flexibility. But all nibs, whether made of gold or of less forgiving, less desirable stainless steel, give fountain pens their distinctive touch and feel, and their unique writing variations. It is the pens' nibs that give writers and their pens a distinctive flair, the elegance of finely shaped notes. Attuned to the disparate angles by which a pen is held, and to all the changes in hand pressure, nibs are the most personal part of the pen. That is why the experts caution against lending your fountain pen to anyone who is not already familiar with using one. For the writer and the nib have a special bond, a connection that extends to the paper, and inspires—or allows—the words to flow smoothly.

But subjected to unremitting hand pressure and to the corrosive effects of ink, nibs are particularly susceptible to cracking, clogging, becoming snarled in cheap paper, and losing their original shape. To avoid some common problems, gold nibs are a far better choice than cheaper stainless steel. Gold is more resistant to corrosive inks, and because it's more malleable than steel, the feel of a gold-nibbed pen affords greater flexibility and smoothness. But a gold nib is delicate and vulnerable, so be careful not to drop a pen on its tip. And ease up; don't apply excessive pressure on any kind of nib.

Don't spend $70 to $200 on a premium nib, then use it on coarse paper, because the fine shreds and dust could get into the nib slit and clog the ink channel. On such rough surfaces, nibs can lose their straightness, or their iridium tips could crack, and that may require a visit to the repair shop. If a common or relatively inexpensive nib must be repaired, amateur do-it-yourselfers can try to fix the problems. But rare, extremely fragile, and vintage nibs ought to be taken to a professional.

When purchasing a vintage pen, carefully inspect the nib to determine if it is scratched or cracked. The best defense against buying damaged items is a magnifying glass, a jeweler's loupe, and a strong light source. Nibs must be kept clean and gleaming. But don't use metal polishes or chemicals to make them sparkle; polishing will take any plating right off. Solid gold nibs with no plating can be polished with Simichrome (a special metal polish that leaves a thin, protective coating to prevent tarnishing), but never use it on a plated nib. Instead, clean these nibs with a dust-free cotton cloth—dampen with water if necessary. If the nib is really dirty, first clean with soapy water. After cleaning or flushing your pen, don't use a rough or lint-covered cloth to dry the nib; that could scratch it. Use tissue paper instead.

The Barrel: The Mysteries of Hard Rubber

The main hard rubber (or even plastic) body of a fountain pen is often vividly colored, marbleized, or exquisitely adorned with a silver or gold overlay. It's the part that pays tribute to design excellence, seduces us, and persuades pen lovers to give up their ballpoints. But, as is so often the case, bewitching beauty is prone to the ravages of time. Rubber discolors. Plastics deteriorate. Both lose their brilliance when continually exposed to bright light, and both are plagued by heat and humidity. Various chemicals, such as the sulfur in inks, can spoil surfaces. Water, if a pen is immersed in it, is another potential troublemaker.

Storing pens properly, away from direct sunlight, can alleviate some problems. As with cigars kept in humidors, pens should be allowed to breathe. They must not be kept, according to expert Richard Binder, in airtight, airless containers or in plastic bags. As he points out, chemicals from these bags can damage the pens' external finish.

Sulfur can be especially harmful, although it is in the latex that is used to make pens. When manufactured rubber comes into contact with water, small amounts of the sulfur in the material will leech out and form small amounts of sulfuric acid inside the barrel, which is very destructive. This acid will discolor celluloid pens, leak into the ink and cause discoloration in the cap, and also tarnish gold nibs. David Nishimura notes that many collectors remove the ink sacs from early or vintage pens and replace them with plastic sacs. Alternatively, collectors can put bits of anti-tarnish paper inside a pen barrel to absorb the sulfur, and to consequently safeguard the rubber and silver accents. Those rubber sacs are extremely problematic. Acutely vulnerable to deteriorating over time, sacs can harden, turn soft, or become filled with holes that disrupt a consistent ink supply. Temperature and humidity can also have a harmful effect on sacs, and these rubber ink reservoirs must be replaced often to ensure a regular flow of ink in vintage pens.

Other elements of the filler assembly, particularly the pressure bar that works in concert with the rubber sac, are also corroded by ink. They must be inspected on a regular basis and cleaned to guarantee smooth operation.

Pen enthusiasts should be equally attentive when handling a pen's threaded section. Don't ever use excessive force. Pens are resilient, but they must still be treated gently. This will enhance their beauty, and lead to a pride of ownership that just might inspire masterful writing. ◨

2

THE BATTLE FOR FOUNTAIN PEN SUPREMACY: 1890–1920

As America consolidated its frontiers and began to assert both international and technological supremacy in the late nineteenth century, feathery goose and turkey quill pens that had worked magic for the likes of Benjamin Franklin and Washington Irving began to seem sorely out of place. Many inventors tried to design pens that carried their own supply of ink and would not need to be continually dipped into bottles or portable inkwells. They experimented with various **ink delivery systems**, and by the 1870s steel-point pens with long, thin rubber reservoirs were touted as "revolutionary" smooth writing instruments.

Now mere historical curiosities found in antiques shops and on the Internet, these early attempts at patenting serviceable fountain pens were commercial

Parker Duofolds and True Blue circa 1928

Parker Duofold Junior Pencils from the Late 1920s

disasters. They not only failed to write, but these steel "self-filling" pens often left pools of spilled ink. According to the folklore surrounding this triumph of American innovation, one day an insurance broker named Lewis Edson Waterman was with a client who was about to sign some contracts. Waterman handed the client a reservoir pen, which refused to write, whereupon the man shook the pen vigorously, triggering a splattering gush of ink. The documents were ruined, and, fearing this was a bad omen, the client stalked out of Waterman's office, vetoing the deal with a string of profanities.

Humiliated, Waterman purportedly retreated to his brother's upstate New York home, where he invented an ink-feed system that essentially used air pressure to guarantee a continuous flow of ink. Adding an air hole in the nib (or point) and three groove-cut channels inside the tubular feed mechanism, Waterman developed a piston-like device that enabled the point to move back and forth from the feed. He patented this ink-air exchange system in 1884 and called the pen the **Waterman Ideal**. Developed before the advent of more technologically advanced filling mechanisms, these hugely successful and "miraculously" portable pens were filled with a simple dropper, and they are generically called **eyedroppers**.

Lewis Waterman, the "father of the modern-day fountain pen," went on to score another commercial triumph in the early 1900s. Realizing that calling his pen the Ideal was a bit of an overstatement (as it leaked after extensive usage), Waterman entered the then fiercely competitive **safety pen** market with his own retractable-nib model. (An *S* after the model number distinguishes these pens, along with goldfilled barrel bands and silver filigree overlays.) By twisting the end of this eyedropper-filled pen, the point moved in and out of the barrel, and to reduce leakage, the **Safety** featured a screw-on cap. These pens wrote smoothly, but at a time when Americans were increasingly mobile, they still required that people carry messy eyedroppers.

The dawning automobile era demanded technological change. But in the scramble to develop the first self-filling pen, the Waterman Company (not to be confused with A. A. Waterman, which produced eminently collectible floral pattern pens under this name and the Chicago Safety brand) lagged behind such pen manufacturers as Conklin, Parker, and Sheaffer. By 1897 Conklin had pioneered the **crescent filler**, an attractive metal overlay pen equipped with a rubber ink sac that is still avidly pursued by collectors. Parker patented the **button filler** in 1905, and Sheaffer soon followed with a **lever filler** that became very successful. But even as pen makers began experimenting with new materials (particularly celluloid in the 1920s), Waterman was unable to perfect an efficient

Parker
Duofold
Chinese
Lacquer Red
1928

Parker
Duofold Big
Reds circa
1988 and circa
1928

self-filler, though it offered four different mechanisms from the late 1890s to 1915.

As David Nishimura suggests on his web site, because these abortive attempts had relatively short commercial runs, their limited production makes each model quite rare. Only a few nineteenth-century **syringe fillers** have ever surfaced, yet Waterman's **pump fillers** dating back to 1910 are available (in the $600 range), as are filigreed **sleeve fillers** with sterling silver overlays ($2,300 to $2,800). These elegant pens predate the extremely rare and difficult to manipulate **coin fillers**, which were filled by inserting a coin into a slot cut in the barrel. Nishimura especially likes Waterman's eyedroppers. As he explains,

"While, for most collectors, eyedroppers are primarily of historical and aesthetic interest, they are eminently functional writing instruments."

It wasn't until 1915 that Waterman finally mounted a **lever filler** (usually nickel- or gold-plated) on the side of the barrel. This device was flipped to a 90-degree angle with a fingernail to empty any remaining ink in the sac, and then flipped back once the point was inserted into an ink bottle. Nishimura says Waterman hard rubber lever fillers are "handsome, solidly built pens with excellent nibs." Such a user-friendly pen made lever fillers popular, but because Sheaffer had pioneered this mechanism, Waterman was seen as an also-ran in the race to develop a truly portable pen. Yet Waterman's reasonably priced 1920s lever fillers have become prized collectibles, particularly red-and-black swirled wood-grain **Cardinal** and **Ripple** pens that are in fine condition.

Waterman was further eclipsed during World War I (1914–1918) when Parker's **Trench** pen (with a compartment for powdered or tablet-form ink) greatly appealed to soldiers. Parker took the lead in 1921, as Rick Conner's Penoply web site points out, as it moved away from traditional, reed-slender black rubber pens and offered red, orange, mandarin yellow, and other brightly colored **Duofolds** that suited the soaring spirits of the 1920s. For instance, the $7 Duofold **Big Red** was used by Sir Arthur Conan Doyle in the writing of Sherlock Holmes's adventures. These flamboyant, oversized pens were such a commercial phenomenon that other companies were forced to respond. Sheaffer introduced the plastic **Jade Senior** in 1924 with an unprecedented lifetime guarantee and, along with rival Eversharp, increasingly used celluloid—a light, unbreakable material that could be fashioned into a variety of colors.

The era of the drab black fountain pen was over, and although Waterman later regained some of its former luster when a French subsidiary pioneered the first **disposable cartridge pen** in 1936, its dominance came to an unceremonious end during the years of the Great Depression (circa 1929–late 1930s). At that time, many companies struggled with debt and folded. But because of the fanfare surrounding those still highly collectible Duofolds and other innovative offerings, Parker became the ruling trendsetter, the visionary force spurring the advent of a golden age of pens.

Price List: 1890–1920

Because of the rich and diverse array of fountain pen models, the collector is confronted by a wide number of ink-fill systems and decorative features. It is therefore crucial to understand the abbreviations that are used on web sites and in retailers' catalogs.

These are the most common abbreviations:

AF   Aerometric Filler

BCHR   Black Chased Hard Rubber

BF   Button Filler

BHR   Black Hard Rubber

CF   Crescent Filler

CPT   Chrome-Plated Trim

ED   Eyedropper

EXC   Excellent Condition

GD   Good Condition

GF   Gold Filled

GFF   Gold-Filled Filigree

GFO Gold-Filled Overlay

GFT Gold-Filled Trim

HR Hard Rubber

K Karat

LF Lever Filler

NM Near Mint Condition

PF Pump Filler

RHR Red Hard Rubber

RMHR Red Mottled Hard Rubber

SF Sleeve Filler

STSL Sterling Silver

TF Twist Filler

VG Very Good Condition

The following price guide lists a sampling of pens produced in the 1900s to the early 1920s. Brief pen descriptions are included, along with the following abbreviated names of reputable, well-established retailers who have at one point sold a particular pen (see "Pen Pals" in the Resource Guide for contact information). It must be noted that prices fluctuate, and it is best to contact the dealers for current market values.

- **BER** Berliner Pens
- **DN** David Nishimura Vintage Pens
- **EB** eBay
- **FPH** Fountain Pen Hospital
- **GP** GoPens
- **1001** 1001Pens
- **PEN** Penopoly
- **PH** PenHome

A. A. Waterman
GF repoussé *floral design, TF, 1910, NM*   *$1,295, FPH*

A. A. Waterman
TF, 1905, GFO, diamond and snail
pattern, exc   *$1,250, DN*

A. A. Waterman
*TF, 1910, GFF slip cap, HR, glossy finish,
fine-exc* $900, DN

A. A. Waterman
TF, 1897–1920, wide band $275, 1001

A. A. Waterman
*TF, 1912 GFF slip cap, "1912" on cap crown,
14.8 cm long, vg to fine* $750, DN

A. A. Waterman
*TF, GF hand-engraved floral pattern slip cap,
marked "Not Connected with the L.E. Waterman
Co." vg to fine* $800, DN

A. A. Waterman
*TF, 39M-3, circa 1920, BCHR, clipless vest pocket,
black and glossy, imprints include "Not Connected
with the L.E. Waterman Co." exc* $105, DN

Aiken Lambert
*Dome Pen, 1915, BCHR, SF, 13.5 cm long, slip
cap marked "Dome Pen/San Francisco," crisp
and glossy, exc-nm* $205, DN

Aiken Lambert
*Retracting Dip Pen, 1880, Oversize, ebonized
wood taper, exc* $500, DN

Betzler
*Early eyedropper, 1900, with mother-of-pearl,
ED, nm* $750, BER

Conklin
#2, CF $895, FPH

Conklin
*#3, 1920, GF CF, quatrefoil floral pattern,
13 cm, lock ring slightly chipped, gd-vg* $600, DN

Conklin
*S3, 1912, BCHR slip cap CF, 13.3 cm long,
strong imprints and chasing, Mark Twain
used this model, fine to exc* $265, DN

Conklin
*#30 crescent fill in BCHR, 1918, GFT, deep
black pen with no ambering, nm* $195, GP

Conklin
*GNL, 1915, large BCHR clipless CF, 13.5 cm,
GFT, one of scarcest sizes, early narrow feed,
scratchy nib, gd* $425, DN

Conklin
*#2, 1920, GFF overlay ringtop, CF, 11.4 cm
HR, black and glossy, metal near perfect,*

near invisible hairline at base of #2 Conklin nib,
exc-nm $450, DN

Conklin
70P, 1917, BCHR, large-sized CF, vg $400, PEN

Conklin
50P, 1917, BCHR, large-sized CF, vg $250, PEN

Conklin
S5, 1910, CF, smooth BHR, slip cap No. 5,
original nib and "Conk-Clip" imprints
readable, vg-exc $498, PH

Dictator
SF, 1915, smooth GFO ringtop, uses ink
pellets or fills conventionally, fine $280, DN

Edward Todd
#5 LF in 16k gold-plated, 1920, alternating
pinstripe and plain panels, indicia engraved
"G.E.H.," cap band engraved "For Exceptional
Service . . . Paramount Theatre, N.Y.," nm $250, GP

Foley
Retractable pocket dip pen, 1872, unmarked,
GF barrel, 1872 dated gold nib, vg $110, DN

French Safety Pen
1920s, no name on pen, STSL overlay on BHR,
extra fine $425, 1001

Gold Starr
Safety, 1920, boxed set, red mottled hard
rubber $185, 1001

James
Safety Pen, 1920, RMHR, ED, fine $95, 1001

Jaxon
Self-Filling, 1915, unusually large BCHR
clipless stud filler, made under Conklin
patent, unlinked, crisp imprints, large nib $200, DN

Mabie Todd & Co.
Engraving on overlay, 1915, gold nib, gd $465, 1001

Mabie Todd & Co.
Unmarked Mercury Glass Dipper, 1890,
fully intact glass nib, perfect condition $75, DN

Mabie Todd & Co.
Swan #2 LF ringtop in STSL, 1920, alternating
vertical pinstripe and vine panels, few surface
scratches, exc $85, GP

Mabie Todd & Co.
Swan self-filler, 1920, 18k solid gold overlay,
clipless LF, grouped parallel lines pattern,

13.3 cm long, few pinpricks around lever end,
stub nib, vg $650, DN

Mabie Todd & Co.
Swan straight cap ED, 1910, 13.5 cm, barleycorn
pattern, New York production, typical corrosion
to section overlay, gd $220, DN

Mabie Todd & Co.
Swan ED, 1890, GF fine barleycorn ED,
overfeed, early markings for Mabie Todd & Bard,
engraved "Dr. E. Dalton," exc-nm $820, DN

Mabie Todd & Co.
Swan Military Safety, 1918, rare screw cap, BCHR,
ED, 14.3 cm, GFT, ink pellet compartment at
end of barrel, New York production, gd $305, DN

Mabie Todd & Co.
Swan, gold-filled straight cap ED, 1912, 13.2 cm,
overfeed nib, unusual lined checkerboard chasing,
New York made, few small barrel dings,
fine-exc $750, DN

Mabie Todd & Co.
Blackbird, 1914, slip cap clipless BCHR, ED,
13.3 cm, New York production, strong imprints
and chasing, slight fading, responsive nib $145, DN

Mabie Todd & Co.
Swan safety, 1918, rare BHR desk style, clipless screw cap,
ED, 17.3 cm, imprints heavily worn, rare, gd $375, DN

Moore
Non-leak Safety, 1917, silver overlay retracting nib pen,
11.3 cm long, grouped parallel lines pattern,
scattered light marks to overlay, vg $825, DN

Moore
#5 Safety in BHR, 1908, repoussé GF barrel, extremely rare,
early model with short flat cap, in original hinged velvet-
lined case, mint $750, GP

Moore
#2 Safety, 1920, fully covered GF pinstriped cap and
barrel, with smooth ends offset with repoussé bands,
hand-engraved vine pattern on barrel under cap,
mint in original hinged velvet-lined case $900, GP

Moore
Midget non-leakable Safety, 1915, BCHR, checkerboard
chasing, GF ringtop and cap crown, "Quick Turn"
cap, exc $150, DN

Mordan
Dip pen and pencil set in box, 1890, smooth
STSL, 15.3 cm long, exc-nm $385, DN

Parker

23H, 1902, BHR, ED, 13.8 cm long, hexagonal body,
iridium missing from one tine of keyhole vent
in Lucky Curve nib, fine-exc $1,100, DN

Parker

46 with mother-of-pearl, extremely rare, 1906–14,
contact for price/availability, PEN

Parker

47 Pregnant Parker, 1905–14, extremely rare, beautiful
overlay and mother-of-pearl slabs, faceted, cap floral design
(surrounded by tendrils of ferns), gold barrel, Parker Lucky
Curve nib, contact for price/availability, PEN

Parker

#24, 1912, rare slip cap, BF with GF "disappearing clip,"
14 cm, quite worn, sealed hairline above clip
opening, scratchy #4 nib, fair to gd $650, DN

Parker

#15, BHR ED, 13.5 cm, GFF cap, beautiful fluted rosy pearl
slabs on barrel, fully marked, nice glossy HR, clean estate
purchase, fine-exc $3,200, DN

Parker

Black Giant ED, 1918, BHR, rare version with large cap,
imprint "Parker Black Giant," cap has a 1" L-shaped
crack, reinforced by wide cap band, exc $950, GP

Parker

Black Giant ED, 1918, BHR, superb condition,
nm $1,500, GP

Parker

Lucky Curve, 1915, Jack Knife Safety ED, "Scroll
and Line" pattern, "pinched waist" design, BHR,
decent condition, some wear, working $295, EB

Parker

Lucky Curve, 1920, GF BF ringtop, nice clean pen,
greenish gold finish, smooth rose gold Lucky
Curve nib, fine $245, DN

Parker

#16 GF filigree over BHR, 1912, ringtop, Lucky
Curve #3 nib, BF, vg $550, PEN

Parker

Giant, 1910, BCHR with wide GF cap band,
extremely large pen (second-largest ever
made by company), 11-1/2" long, exc $5,000, PEN

Parker

46, 1905, BHR with mother-of-pearl panels around the body,
cap is GF taper with a snail pattern, rare beautiful design,

mother-of-pearl panels susceptible to damage, so not many exist in good condition today, exc $10,000, PEN

Parker
Duofold Junior Lucky Curve, 1916, green marbleized, top half lighter green, bottom half darker green, push-button PF, bladder needs to be replaced, otherwise gd condition $30, EB

Sheaffer
Black Bakelite, gold trim, 5-1/2" long, solid gold clip, needs new sac, good $31, EB

Sheaffer
#2 LF pen and pencil set, 1917, GF mint pen in original box $145, GP

Sheaffer
46 Special, 1920, BCHR, LF ringtop, 11.9 cm GFT, unusual grouped wavy lines chasing, crisp and glossy, nm $205, DN

Sheaffer
Craig, 1920, BHR LF, 11.6 cm GF ringtop, nickel lever, named after Walter A. Sheaffer's son and heir, nib has hairline at base, lacks iridium, vg-fine $80, DN

Sheaffer
LF, 1918, BCHR, LF ringtop, distinctive zigzag chasing, crisp and glossy, GF ringtop fitting, exc $90, DN

Sheaffer
LF, 1918, rare super-slender GF full overlay, section covered, 11.8 cm long, longitudinal engine turned panels, "A.C.P.E." rather crudely engraved on barrel, vg-fine $325, DN

Sheaffer
Self-filling, 1918, rare GFF over BHR, ringtop LF, 10.3 cm, HR surface black but dull, fine-exc $650, DN

Sheaffer
Self-filling, 1918, rare slotted pattern, GF overlay over BHR ringtop LF, 10 cm, scratchy nib, fine $675, DN

Sheaffer
LF, 1920, rare GF ringtop, 8.7 cm, gd-vg $145, DN

Sheaffer
Self-filling, 1916, GF LF ringtop, 9.9 cm, BHR section, nm $160, DN

Sheaffer
Self-filling, 1917, STSL filigree over BHR LF, 13.1 cm, silver-plated clip is a replacement or

later addition, crack under cap barely visible,
scarce pen $750, DN

Sheaffer
Ringtop red hard rubber, 1922, 3-3/8" long,
LF, exc $400, PEN

Wahl
Tempoint, 1918, scarce early GF overlay LF,
11.1 cm long, roller clip, check pattern, small
nicks on cap, otherwise crisp, fine-exc $200, DN

Wahl
Tempoint, 1919, early STSL LF ringtop,
9.5 cm, no Wahl marks, only Boston Safety
patent dates, grouped parallel line ribbon
pattern, vg-fine $95, DN

Wahl
Tempoint, 1920, GF "all metal barrel" LF, in
crisp Colonial pattern (fine parallel line), fine $200, DN

Waterman
20, 1907, RHR with black speckles, only
three known to exist, slip cap, nm $60,000, PEN

Waterman
418, 1907, RHR with fine silver overlay, art
deco design, rare to have large model with
silver overlay, uncommon in red,
slip cap, exc $40,000, PEN

Waterman
412, 1917, fine silver, high-relief rose design,
extremely rare because of high-relief design,
mint $8,500, PEN

Waterman
45, 1912, sterling silver, Safety pen, line/dot/line
pattern is rare, exc $5,000, PEN

Waterman
42, 1915, 18k rolled gold overlay, Safety pen,
overlay is French in origin, exc $4,000, PEN

Waterman
Doll's Pen, 1907, BHR, very rare with original
box, smallest pen known to have ever been
made, 2-1/2" long but useable, mint $5,500, PEN

Waterman
416 Sterling, 1910, rare and large, early ED slip cap,
STSL filigree overlay, art nouveau pattern,
original 14k nib, some wear, exc $300 range, EB

Waterman
STSL filigree overlay, 1909, art nouveau pattern,
LF, nm $1,500, BER

Waterman
Gold-filled "Golph" design overlay, 1905 $825, FPH

Waterman
Red mottled hard rubber #13, 1905, red $249, 1001

Waterman
BCHR, 1915, fair $120, 1001

Waterman
#18 mottled transition hard rubber, 1905,
ED, nm $1,500, BER

Waterman
#14, 1906, ED, black, gold clip and emblem,
in Waterman box $300, 1001

Waterman
#15, ED, wide chased bands, gd, in box $295, 1001

Waterman
Ideal New York, #12, 1900, wide gold band,
leather box $250, 1001

Waterman
0502 ED 18, gold filled, golpheresque pattern
(heavy gold plate brocade), nm $950, GP

Waterman
The Doll's Pen, very small size, very rare
model in black HR, nm, limited number
made $3,500, GP

Waterman
#42 Safety pen, 1917, 18k rolled gold, pinstriped
pattern, nm $675, GP

Waterman
#442 1/2 Safety pen, 1920, STSL on BHR,
Xs with pinstriped pattern, nm $400, GP

Waterman
#402 straight holder, 1900, ED in STSL,
smooth finish, rare model, nm $1,100, EB

Waterman
402, 1903, rare short model, 11 cm, STSL
fine barleycorn ED, English hallmarks, 1904,
hairline crack in section mouth, vg $685, DN

Waterman
12 1/2, 1910, RHR, clipless slender ED, some
scratches on cap, fine-exc $875, DN

Waterman
412 VS, 1912, BHR safety, STSL filigree, 11.9 cm,
unusual early mechanism, nib turns as extends
and retracts, very clean, fine-exc $850, DN

Waterman
#13, 1912, scarce #3 size BHR, slip cap ED,
side clip with German Silver imprint, fine $245, DN

Waterman
#14, 1915, unusual BCHR clipless ED, wide GF
cap band with red and white enamel emblem
for Leander Clark College of Toledo, Iowa,
strong chasing, fine-exc $225, DN

Waterman
12, 1915, mottled HR, ED, 13.6 cm, fine color,
fine-exc $175, DN

Waterman
12VS, 1918, early Italian overlaid Continental ringtop
GF safety, engine turned panels and bands of
vegetal decoration, seems to hold ink, vg-fine $585, DN

Waterman
0512 1/2 NS Baby, 1918, smooth GFO safety with
rare double cap, virtually no plating wear
but inner cap dinged, vg-fine $450, DN

Waterman
412 SF filigree, 1908, rare SF with STSL overlay,
14.1 cm, metal crisp, exc $275, DN

Waterman
0512, SF filigree, SF, 1912, GFO, only slightest
fading, metal exc with minimal brassing, clean
example of a rare and interesting pen, fine $2,250, DN

Waterman
12PSF, STSL overlay, BHR, swastika design exc,
contact for price, PEN

Waterman
454 filigree, BHR, STSL overlay, 1920s,
LF, exc $350, PEN

Waterman
0-552 filigree, BHR, GF overlay, 1920s,
LF, exc $350, PEN

Waterman
452 1/2V, pen/pencil set, LF, ringtop, vg $200, PEN

Waterman
55, BHR, 14k Waterman #5 nib, cap is crisp
in exc condition, barrel good condition $150, PEN

Waterman
52 1/2V, red wood grain, ringtop, LF,
14k nib, exc-nm $140, PEN

Waterman
12S Safety, BCHR, exc chasing and imprints,
4-11/16", exc $150, PEN

Waterman

55V, 1919, smooth BHR ringtop, 12 cm, GF,
crisp and glossy, nm $265, DN

Waterman

#12 ED, 1899, red mottled hard rubber 12 pen,
extra fine, in box $250, 1001

Waterman

0515POC, 1920, ED, GF overlay over BHR,
rare model, exc $1,303, PH

Waterman

12P, 1910, BCHR PF, 14.8 cm, good imprints
with 1897 and 1900 patent dates, moderate
even fading, nice example of one of Waterman's
earliest and least successful self-fillers, fine $675, DN

Waterman

504 straight holder in 18k, 1900, alternating line,
dot, and barley panels, nm $3,000, assorted retailers

Waterman

0314 ED, 1905, BCHR, GF chased filigree
overlay, very rare, nm, in original hinged velvet-
lined case $900, GP

Waterman

#13 ED, BCHR, barrel and cap evenly ambered,
extremely rare model, crisp chasing
and imprint $125, GP

Waterman

(5)12 Safety, 1910, 18k heavy fluted overlay,
very rare, nm $1,100, GP

Waterman

(05) 52V LF, 1915, 18k Italian-crafted overlay,
pinstripe/diamond panels, no dents or
dings, nm $275, GP

Waterman

552 LF set in 9k barley overlay. 1915, Indicia
engraved "W.H.T.P." Samuel Mordan
9k matching pencil, cap is BHR with GF
clip and imprinted "Waterman's made in
USA," set created quite a stir in London
as it documents that Mordan, a famous
UK jeweler, manufactured pencils for
Waterman, mint in box $1,200, GP

Waterman

Lady Patricia LF set in GF Basketweave, nm $600, GP

Waterman

(05) 42 Continental Safety in 18k, 1917, wide
"Dancing Cherub" panels on cap and band, as
well as wide filigree and repoussé panels, cap

has a winged nib, the hallmark of Capra
Guiseppi (Milan) the Italian importer of
Waterman pens, incredibly beautiful, nm $2,500, GP

Unmarked
ED, 1905, BHR, GF scroll filigree overlay,
14k nib, very gd to fine $225, DN

Unmarked
ED, 1915, clipless screw cap, GFO, hand
engraved with flowers and scrolling leaves,
minimal wear, fine to exc $500, DN

■

3

MICHELANGELO AND HIS TEMPTATIONS: 1920–1930

Casting a seductive spell with its dazzling gold, emerald-eyed snake atop the cap, and two gold reptiles entwined around a lustrous, jet black, hard rubber body, the **Parker Snake** has long been the world's most coveted pen—and the most difficult to acquire. Using the **lost wax** method of metal casting that was developed by the Shang Dynasty in China, these Snakes are a symphony of 18k gold, impeccably faceted emeralds, and black acrylic. Lost wax or *cire perdue* is a sculptural process of metal casting that may be used for hollow and solid casting, where a sculptor makes a model in plaster or clay that is then coated with wax. As Parker described the reissued Snake in 1997, "Throughout history, the snake or serpent has been held as a respectful symbol of power, life and rebirth."

Sheaffer Balance Jade Oversize 1930 and 3-25 Blue and Black 1932

Mabie Todd Swan Visofil VT Gray and Ladies V Series Green 1936–1939

Here was a pen that epitomized true majesty, the pinnacle of the pen maker's art.

Of course, that distinction could be challenged by the equally alluring **Parker Aztec**, another early-twentieth-century *repoussé* gem embellished with the heads of regal-looking Indian chiefs, their arrows, and intricately detailed jewelry. This Awanyu Indian design was inspired by Parker's visit to Santa Fe, New Mexico, in 1900.

But there's no debating the fact that a schoolteacher from Janesville, Wisconsin, who grew increasingly frustrated with repairing his students' leaky pens, became renowned for unrivaled artistry. Transforming pen-making technology with bold, bewitching designs and engineering innovations (such as the **Vacumatic** and **capillary filler** systems), George S. Parker was the industry's high-wire trapeze artist, a cross between Michelangelo and promotional wizard P. T. Barnum.

In this flamboyant salesman's world, everything from **Red** and **Black Giant** pens to a new filling system, to his tossing "unbreakable" pens from an airplane into the Grand Canyon was heralded as a sensational, newsworthy breakthrough. Parker transformed pen advertising, spending huge sums to promote his latest innovations in newspapers and magazines. Yet before Parker seized the public's imagination and rose to the forefront of stylish, technologically advanced pen manufacturing, this marketing genius had to grapple with the ongoing riddle of the leaky fountain pen.

Before he rather inadvertently became a world-renowned inventor, George S. Parker was a telegraphy teacher, intent on helping his students unravel the mysteries of Morse code. Often asked to repair their pens, Parker realized that when pens were carried in shirt or jacket pockets, the body heat transferred to the pen caused the ink to expand and rush toward the point. Tired of having his teaching interrupted by these messy inconveniences, he developed a **curled feed system** with a locking device that prevented excess ink from reaching the point.

Called the **Parker Lucky Curve**, this 1894-patented pen was widely advertised as a leak-proof. The **capillary action** feed mechanism (draining the excess ink out of the point and back into the sac or reservoir) worked extremely well, and to guarantee its continued commercial success, Parker made sure the company's signature item was used at the signing of the Treaty of Paris that ended the Spanish-American War in 1898.

The country was now at peace, and as the new American century began, Parker was ready to launch other big ideas. His grandest works were the Aztec and the Snake, two exquisitely crafted gold or silver pens that are virtually impossible to acquire because of their limited production and astronomical five-figure price tags. One of these gems will occasionally appear at an auction, but the bidding for them is fierce, and unseasoned collectors might not be ready to delve into such a high-octane environment.

Far more obtainable, the red hard rubber **Duofold** was another huge success, one that moved Parker past Waterman, into first place in sales. The Duofold was Parker's first mass-produced pen and was a major success. The Duofolds appeared in various sizes (the largest one, as Rick Conner points out, was the 10-inch **Pregnant Parker Duofold**, which hid a normal-sized pen under its blind cap) and in a variety of colors (such as lapis lazuli, green and pearl, and burgundy). The original was a reddish orange, usually called **Chinese Lacquer Red** by the company, but dubbed **Big Red** by collectors. Widely advertised in the late 1920s, these large attention-grabbing pens were given the era's popular "Duo" tag to promote their sturdiness and performance. (The many reasons for the "Duo" tag are explored on Conner's Penoply web site.) That marketing embellishment was meant to enhance the manly, statement-making aura of these $7 pens (twice the price of most pens at that time), which had a twenty-five year guarantee. Even today these pens have a robust appeal among collectors.

According to David Nishimura, Big Red, the vivid reddish orange Duofold with a button filler that was pressed down while the point was submerged in the ink supply, is one of the most fiercely pursued pens ever produced. Released in far smaller numbers than the flashy red classic, Parker's 1927 **Mandarin Yellow** model also attracts wide collector interest. It was originally a commercial flop, easily stained and breakable. It featured celluloid instead of hard rubber, and consequently was very brittle. That has made it relatively hard to find, and has boosted the value of pieces without any cracks or discolorations.

Undaunted by the Mandarin's failure, the enterprising Parker went on to pioneer other technological advancements. Typically upstaging his competitors, who were still wrestling with the problematic rubber sacs in their pens (used to store ink, these sacs or tubes quickly deteriorated because of oxidation), he introduced the so-called "sac-less" **Vacumatic** in 1934.

Parker
Vacumatic
Azure Blue
1942–1946 / A
Blue Diamond
Model

Parker
Vacumatic
Golden Web
1936–1937

Showcasing a newly developed fill system with plunger and rubber diaphragm, this highly collectible pen held far more ink than other pens of that era, and its internal diaphragm actually was a type of sac. These pens were made of opaque laminated celluloid that made the ink supply visible, and were offered with two-toned nibs and striking gold-filled caps. Vacumatics are also known as **Golden Arrows** (these distinctive clips have since become a company trademark), and despite Parker's stretching of the truth—it was Sheaffer that developed the first *truly* sac-less pen—Vacumatics were an immediate commercial sensation.

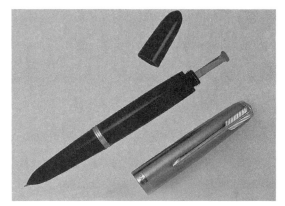

Parker 51
Demi circa
1949

Parker 51
Flighter
1949–1955

Parker 51
Cedar Blue
Vacumatic
circa 1947

Although the Vacumatics dominated the marketplace until the advent of World War II, the public demand for such large pens waned. Always searching for that next big idea—and realizing that war meant a scarcity of production materials—Parker experimented with a lightweight barrel material in the 1930s that would replace celluloid. This new methyl methacrylate resin, as Conner's web site points out, was known as Plexiglas, Lucite, or Acrylic. Debuting in 1941 and produced for thirty years, this strong and easily colored material was used in a classic $12.50 fountain pen that eventually reshaped the competitive battlefield, the **51**.

Honoring the company's fifty-first anniversary, this **double jeweled** pen featured aluminum jewels on the cap and blind cap until 1942, when they were replaced by plastic jewels. Its esoteric-sounding parts such as a *breather tube* and *clutch ring* were pure space age, ingeniously concealing the feed and platinum-tipped point inside a futuristic-looking *jet snout*. Many models were offered, including the **Flighter**, the **Presidential**, the **Demi**, and the **Heirloom**. Conner notes that there was also a "secret weapon" attraction, a collector or feed mechanism that trapped or stored vast quantities of ink without leaking. As Kenneth Parker, president of Parker from the early 1930s to 1960, boasted, "[T]he pen was made to look like someone's idea of a dream pen. It was sleek . . . as well as a good functional pen, a well styled one . . . something that was good to touch and see."

So many aspects of the 51 were technologically advanced (in 1948 an aerometric Pli-glass ink reservoir or filler was added) that the relatively high-priced pen was eventually exhibited in the Museum of Modern Art. Its sleek, streamlined design (often compared to the P-51 Mustang fighter plane) was incorporated into ballpoint and **Liquid Lead** pencils that were also popular by the mid-1950s. Yet the stream of plaudits for the 51 that keeps values high (it is often described as the best fountain pen ever made, and the record holder in terms of highest sales volume, it typically sells for $150 to $700) has also had more sinister repercussions. As pen expert David Nishimura points out, collectors must beware: the 51 is often counterfeited.

Parker 61
Custom Gray
1961–1969

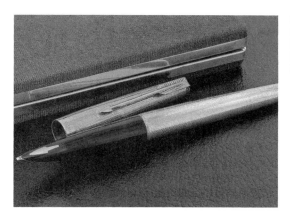

Parker 61
Solid 9 Karat
Waterdrop
Presidential,
Early 1960s

Parker 51 counterfeits are usually easy to spot, however, due to their poor fit and finish. Fortunately, most of the counterfeits made over the years were inexact, and often merely replicas, so it is easy to tell them from the real thing. Many have had Chinese characters, ink-vue windows, and other non-Parker details.

In the 1956 Parker pioneered another scientific breakthrough with the **61**, which was "astronomically priced" at $20 (later 61 models such as the 14-karat **Presidential** sold for $150). Dispensing with all the squeezing, pressing, and lever mechanisms (Conner describes this innovative pen as "no squeezing, no screwing, no levers, no moving parts of any description"), this "revolutionary" capillary filler model simply had to be dropped into a bottle of ink after the barrel was unscrewed, and *voilà*—the pen filled itself. "As if that wasn't cool enough," says Conner, "the 61 also cleaned itself," and featured the same plastic collector mechanism as in the 51.

As ballpoints gained greater popularity in the next few decades, less attention would be paid to advancing fountain pen technology. (See *Chapter 6: The Ballpoint Pen* for more information.) Yet before Parker was acquired by the Gillette Company in 1993, the spirit of its innovative founder was again resurrected in the **T-1**. Made of titanium, a material used by the aerospace industry, this pen was supposed to capture the adventure and excitement of lunar exploration. But despite its gleaming, extremely aerodynamic profile, the T-1 fizzled commercially because of high production costs (only a token number appeared in shops), and the pen's resulting scarcity has led to a dramatic increase in value.

Price List: 1920–1930

Because of the rich and diverse array of fountain pen models, the collector is confronted by a wide number of ink-fill systems and decorative features. It is therefore crucial to understand the abbreviations that are used on web sites and in retailers' catalogs.

These are the most common abbreviations:

- **BCHR** Black Chased Hard Rubber
- **BF** Button Filler
- **BHR** Black Hard Rubber
- **CF** Crescent Filler
- **ED** Eyedropper
- **EXC** Excellent Condition
- **GD** Good Condition
- **GF** Gold Filled
- **GFO** Gold-Filled Overlay
- **GFT** Gold-Filled Trim
- **HR** Hard Rubber
- **K** Karat
- **LF** Lever Filler

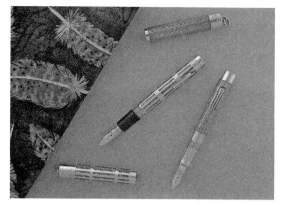

A Set of Wahl-Eversharp Gold-Filled and Vermeil Ringtops from the 1920s

Wahl-Eversharp Coronet circa 1937 and Commander Showing Use of Similar Plastics

- **NM** Near Mint Condition
- **PF** Pump Filler
- **PNF** Pneumatic Filler
- **RHR** Red Hard Rubber
- **STSL** Sterling Silver
- **TF** Twist Filler
- **VG** Very Good Condition

The following price guide lists a sampling of pens produced by Parker and other major companies during the 1920s and early '30s. Brief pen descriptions are included along with the abbreviated names of the following reputable, well-established retailers who have at some point sold a particular pen (see "Pen Pals" in the Resource Guide, for contact information). It must be noted that prices fluctuate, and it is best to contact the dealers for current market values.

- **BER** Berliner Pens
- **DN** David Nishimura Vintage Pens
- **EB** eBay
- **FPH** Fountain Pen Hospital
- **GP** GoPens
- **1001** 1001Pens
- **PEN** Penopoly
- **PH** PenHome

Chilon
Wingflow, 1936, black plastic with GF inserts, unique art deco design, a regional distributor that never had wide distribution, vg　　　$600, PEN

Chilton
PNF, 1928, black ringtop, 14k solid gold cap band, exc　　　$200, DN

Chilton
PNF, 1925, GFT, 11.3 cm long, exc　　　$265, DN

Conklin
Crescent Endura Transition #6, 1924, red and black mottled HR section, original 14k nib, nm　　　$2,000, EB

Conklin
Endura Standard, 1926, LF, sapphire blue, GFT, nm　　　$225, GP

Conklin
Lever filler, 1925, small lined BHR ringtop, LF, 9 cm, fine-exc　　　$80, DN

Conklin
Endura Symetrik Oversize, 1930, LF in black and bronze, GFT, large pen　　　$550, GP

Conklin
Endura large LF in black, 1927, GFT, rare model with narrow clip band, nm　　　$475, GP

Conway Stewart
ED in BCHR, 1925　　　$295, PH

Conway Stewart
ED, 1925, very rare in chased BHR, vg-exc　　　$330, PH

Conway Stewart
Duro 30, 1930, BF, uncommon to find BF in BHR, rare No. 30, vg-exc　　　$330, PH

Dunn
BHR, PF, 1921, nm $395, FPH

Eclipse
LF, 1927, full size, GFO, Criterion brand clip,
iridium on nib, fine $165, DN

Eversharp
Doric, TF, 4 9/16", adjustable nib with ink
shutoff valve, exc $175, PEN

Eversharp
Doric, black plastic, 4 3/4", vg $125, PEN

Gold Medal
LF, 1930, black and pearl, LF ringtop, GFT,
small nib, exc $85, DN

Le Boeuf
40 Unbreakable, 1926, dark blue and ivory
longitudinally striped, LF ringtop, 10.7 cm long,
GF, fine to exc $200, DN

Le Boeuf
40 Unbreakable, 1926, blue-on-blue swirl,
LF, GFT, gd $115, DN

Mabie Todd & Co.
Swan GF LF, 1925, 13 cm pattern with
panels of wavelike engine turning, New
York production, covered section, fine line
of brassing at end of barrel, fine condition $300, DN

Mabie Todd & Co.
Swan self-filler, 1925, smooth BHR, clipless
LF, 12.7 cm, GFT, vg $85, assorted contacts

Mabie Todd & Co.
Swan SM 205/63, 1927, LF in russet and
jade, unusual color, GFT, nm plus $300, GP

Mabie Todd & Co.
Swan #4 Leverless, 1932, blue marble,
GFT, inlaid GF swan in crown, nm $235, GP

Mabie Todd & Co.
Swan 44 Eternal, 1925, LF, jade color, nm $200, GP

Mabie Todd & Co.
46 Eternal, 1927, LF, near mint $400, GP

Montblanc
Number 1 Safety, 1925, GF Italian overlay,
smallest safety filler $2,400, PH

Montblanc
C Series III, 1932, black and pearl bandless,
GFT, BF $1,575, FPH

Montblanc
*No. 1 Safety, Germany, 1925, one of the
smallest safety fillers, GF Italian overlay,
cap cartouche imprint, vg-exc* $2,400, PH

Montblanc
Lever filler #4, 1920–30, STSL filigree, fine $9,275, 1001

Montblanc
Cardinal Red #40, 1930, red plastic, good $1,200, 1001

Montblanc
#6 Safety pen, 1920s, GF repoussé design $11,000, 1001

Montblanc
#7 BHR, 1920s, good $8,550, 1001

Montblanc
*#30 Masterpiece push knob filler, 1930, in
coral red, GFT, wonderful condition, just
tad of barrel imprint wear* $800, GP

Montblanc
*136 Meisterstück PIF, 1937, in black with long
barrel window, GFT, imprint worn off inner cap,
otherwise nm* $600, GP

Montblanc
Long Safety, 1925, BHR $875, 1001

Parker
#16, GFO over BHR, 1918, BF exc $435, FPH

Parker
*Senior Streamlined Duofold, 1930, Mandarin
Yellow, BF, Lucky Curve nib, exc* $1,495, FPH

Parker
*Duofold Lucky Curve Senior, Mandarin
Yellow, 1927, BF* $1,515, PH

Parker
*Duofold Senior, 1922, RHR bandless, very
clean specimen, 9 mm sealed hairline to
cap lip, stub nib, exc* $950, DN

Parker
*Duofold Senior, Big Red, 1926, BF in cardinal,
GFT, bit of brassing, exc plus* $195, GP

Parker
*Duofold Senior, Big Red Duofold pen and
pencil, 1927, extra fine* $695, 1001

Parker
*Duofold, 1927–29, black permanite, gold nib,
fine* $400, 1001

Parker
Mandarin Yellow Duofold, 1927, good $330, 1001

Parker
Pastel BF ringtop, 1926, coral (rare color),
GFT, a tad of brassing at bottom edge of
cap band, exc $100, GP

Parker
Senior Duofold set, 1926, lapis blue plastic,
early flat-top model, color susceptible to
darkening, but this set has near original
color, exc $950, PEN

Parker
Duofold Senior Streamline, 1929, BF in lapis
blue, GFT, barrel a shade darker than cap,
crisp imprint, no brassing $495, GP

Parker
Lady Duofold, 1927, BF ringtop in black, GFT,
rare model, tad of imprint wear, otherwise nm $125, GP

Parker
Duofold Senior, 1928, BF in mandarin yellow,
GFT, beautiful pen with great color, no cracks
or brassing, nm $1,500, GP

Parker
Duofold Junior, 1924, BF in cardinal, BHR,
very rare, some brassing, exc plus $250, GP

Parker
Duofold Junior Deluxe, 1923, scarce RHR BF with
wide gold-filled cap band, large barrel imprint,
like-new condition but trace of brassing,
exc-nm $395, DN

Parker
Moire, 1929, pale apple green BF ringtop, 11.5 cm,
GFT, crisp end milling, fine color, slight barrel
discolor, exc $135, DN

Parker
Lucky Curve, 1929, long slender black BF,
13.2 cm, GFT, smooth Lucky Curve nib, exc $245, DN

Parker
Duofold Junior, 1927, mandarin yellow,
BF, nm $400, BER

Parker
Duofold Senior, 1922, RHR, unusual wide flush
4.5 mm "Golden Girdle" cap band, chipping
to threads under blind cap, firm nib, fine $705, DN

Parker
Duofold Junior, 1925, RHR BF, single raised
cap band, fine-exc $220, DN

Parker
Lucky Curve, 1925, rose GF BF, 10.8 cm, nice
clean pen, fine $275, DN

Parker
D.Q. 1925 BHR "Duofold quality" BF,
13.6 cm, slightly faded, hairline in smooth
Lucky Curve nib, vg-fine $120, DN

Parker
D.Q., 1925 BHR, "Duofold quality" BF,
13.6 cm, crisp group lines chasing, original
price band, HR faded to medium olive, original
hardened sac has not been replaced $100, DN

Parker
Jack Knife Safety, 1925, GF filigree ringtop BF,
11.7 cm long, metal crisp and fully marked,
HR black and glossy, smooth Lucky Curve
nib, exc-nm $600, DN

Parker
Duofold Senior Lucky Curve Deluxe,
1928, black $880, PH

Parker
VP Holy Water Sprinkler, black, GF cap, exc
                    contact for price/availability, PEN

Parker
Lucky Curve pen/pencil set, 1920, in GF metal,
original box, BF, exc
                    contact for price/availability, PEN

Parker
Duofold Junior Lucky Curve, 1925, BF,
18k gold nib, rare French engine turned
overlay $2,245, PH

Parker
Duofold Lucky Curve, 1927, BF, lapis blue $430, PH

Parker
Duofold Senior Lucky Curve, 1929, BF,
jade green, some signs of wear $695, PH

Parker
Duofold Senior Deluxe set, 1929, black lined
pearl BF, 13.8 cm, GFT, pen barrel Canadian
production, rest U.S., crisp imprints, big
Duofold Deluxe firm nib, fine-exc $585, DN

Parker
Duofold Special, 1929–41, black BF, 13.5 cm,
GFT, narrow cap bands, U.S. Specials are
not common, fine-excellent $285, DN

Parker
Duofold Junior, 1932, Streamline BF, jade green, wonderful color, nm $400, DN

Parker
Lady Duofold Deluxe, 1928, orange BF ringtop, 11.9 cm, GFT, wide cap band, exc-nm $150, DN

Parker
Duofold Senior set, 1928–39, unusual late production but using early production parts, barrel with yellow threads, pencil crown has one small ding, fine-exc $2,200, DN

Parker
Duofold Senior, 1927, black BF, single flush cap band, small Lucky Curve imprint, clean pen, fine-exc $375, DN

Parker
Senior Duofold Streamline in black permanite, large Arrow nib, GFT, exc $96, EB

Parker
#152, Big Red Senior Duofold, 1926, raised cap band, no cracks, restored $152, EB

Parker
STSL button filler, "line and scroll" pattern overlay, rare, Lucky Curve, clean, crisp, minimal wear $217, EB

Parker
Duofold Senior, 1925, RHR BF, raised single cap band, good imprint, slight scrape spot on edge of each end piece, exc $650, DN

Parker
Duofold Junior, 1932, burgundy (red, pearl, and black) Streamline BF, 12.1 cm, original hardened sac hasn't been replaced, mint $350, DN

Parker
Duofold BF, senior-sized Lucky Curve, 1929, Duofold in jade green, minor barrel discoloration, vg-exc $695, PH

Parker
Duofold Junior, mandarin yellow, 1928, BF, GFT, nm $1,250, GP

Parker
Duofold BF, 1927, rare single-banded Lucky Curve, Senior in mandarin yellow, good color, crisp imprints $1,515, PH

Parker
Duofold Senior, 1930, BF, green and pearl, exc $650, GP

Parker
*Duofold Lucky Curve, 1927, BF, lapis blue,
reasonably good color, vg-exc*   *$430, PH*

Parker
*Moire ringtop, 1930, BF, in apple green, GFT,
exc*   *$100, EB*

Parker
Duofold Senior, 1927, BF, white on blue, nm   *$750, GP*

Parker
Pastel, BF, in coral, some signs of wear   *$125, GP*

Parker
Bandless, 1921–22, red, fine   *$675, 1001*

Parker
Duofold Lady, 1928, red permanite, BF, nm   *$75, BER*

Parker
*Thrift Time, 1932, BF, in brown cream, GFT,
near exc*   *$150, GP*

Sager Transparo Sackless
*1928, black, Oversize, PF, transparent celluloid
barrel, 14.2 cm long, excellent transparency,
exc-nm*   *$465, DN*

Security
*Giant, 1925, RHR, GFT, 13.7 cm long, crisp
imprints, hairline on barrel, fine*   *$550, DN*

Sheaffer
*Flat Top, 1928, black Radite, plastic,
LF, nm*   *$200, BER*

Sheaffer
*Secretary, 1925, cherry red Radite LF, 11.5 cm
GFT, barrel slightly darker than cap, vg-fine*   *$425, DN*

Sheaffer
*Lifetime, 1927, pale green LF ringtop, GFT,
no white dot, some discoloration, gd-vg*   *$60, DN*

Sheaffer
*Lifetime Autograph Oversize, 1928, black flat
top LF, 13.2 cm GFT with 14k solid gold cap,
engraved "Edith," white dot on cap crown,
fine*   *$320, DN*

Sheaffer
*Lifetime Balance Oversize, 1930, LF, black
and pearl, GFT, nm*   *$375, GP*

Sheaffer
*Lifetime Balance, 1937, black, full size,
GFT, nm*   *$65, GP*

Sheaffer
*Lifetime, 1928–36, jade green LF ringtop,
11.8 cm, GFT white dot at end of barrel,
exc color, strong imprints, exc* $85, DN

Sheaffer
*Balance 5-30, 1929, bright green LF, 13.5 cm
GFT exc color, crisp imprints, long barrel,
short section, exc-nm* $250, DN

Sheaffer
*Lifetime, 1929, black and pearl LF ringtop,
11.9 cm GFT, white dot on side of cap, good
imprints, fine* $85, DN

Sheaffer
*Oversize Autograph Lifetime Balance, 1932,
green pearl and black marble LF, 14k solid
gold clip and cap band, 14 cm, early large
white dot cap band engraved with
signature, exc* $520, DN

Sheaffer
*Oversize Lifetime Balance, 1934, black LF
with inlaid abalone flakes, 13.8 cm, GFT,
large white dot, fine-exc* $395, DN

Sheaffer
*Junior 275, 1935, black with abalone inlay,
LF, 13.8 cm chrome-plated trim, fine-exc* $150, DN

Sheaffer
*Vacuum-Fil, 1935, 3 pens, 3 large plunger fillers,
2 lack nibs, plungers stuck, transparency perfect
on all 3, nm* $385, DN

Sheaffer
*Lifetime Balance, 1925, LF, full size in green
marble, company's best pen, GFT, nm* $100, GP

Sheaffer
*Balance, 1938, brown striated, Oversize
models are in great demand, exc* $350, PEN

Wahl
*LF, 1924, rose GF "all metal barrel" LF ringtop,
"ripple pattern," vg* $95, DN

Wahl
*LF, 1925, GF "all metal barrel" ringtop in
dart pattern, 9.6 cm, fine* $85, DN

Wahl-Eversharp
*Paramount, 1925, BHR Oversize LF, 14 cm,
GFT, original nib, nm* $265, DN

Wahl-Eversharp
*Signature, 1927, RHR LF, GFT, roller clip,
11.9 cm, exc* $400, DN

Wahl-Eversharp
*Gold Seal Signature set in box, 1929, Oversize
black and pearl "Deco Band" Personal Point LF,
13.6 cm, outstanding color and condition,
pencil uses 1.1 mm lead, nm* $1,600, DN

Wahl-Eversharp
*#2 LF, 1927, in rosewood, hard rubber,
GFT, nm* $125, GP

Wahl-Eversharp
*#2 full-length LF, 1927, deep jade, GFT,
roller ball clip, nm* $200, GP

Wahl-Eversharp
*#2 Equipoised full-length LF, 1938, blood red,
very rare, GFT, tad of lever brassing but nm* $435, GP

Wahl-Eversharp
*Doric GS Oversize, 1931, LF in red marble,
GFT, few surface scratches, but nm* $775, GP

Wahl-Eversharp
*#2, 1927, LF, rosewood color, hard rubber,
GFT, nm* $175, GP

Wahl-Eversharp
*#6, 1925, Gold Seal Personal Point in BHR,
LF, cap GF, nm* $345, GP

Wahl-Eversharp
*Ringtop, 1922–23, overlay over black hard
rubber, 14k nib* $125, 1001

Wahl-Eversharp
Clip Pen, 1925, extra-fine overlay on BHR $185, 1001

Waterman
Patrician, 1929, LF, in jade, GFT $1,500, GP

Waterman
*Patrician Transition, 1928, LF, rivet clip,
extremely rare, nm* $1,500, GP

Waterman
*#7, 1927, LF, red ripple with green color
band, rare model, nm* $575, GP

Waterman
*Signagraph, 1924, BHR, used in Wats
Signagraph check-writing machine,
11.3 cm, gd* $105, DN

Waterman
*42 1/2, 1925, BHR safety with GF 18k Italian octagonal
overlay, 12.2 cm, one pinprick ding on each side
of cap, fine* $585, DN

Waterman

72 1/2, 1925, BCHR, clipless screw-cap ED,
12.8 cm, crisp and glossy, nm $175, DN

Waterman

42 1/2, 1925, BHR safety with GF overlay,
French hallmarks, parallel lines pattern,
12.5 cm long, has been recorked, fine $425, DN

Waterman

56 Red Ripple hard rubber, 1926, LF, nm $600, BER

Waterman

42 1/2, 1925, BHR safety with GF Italian octagonal
overlay, 12.2 cm, one pinprick ding on side of cap,
crown slightly flattened, fine $585, DN

Waterman

#452 1/1V, ladies sterling silver ringtop, 1927,
basket weave pattern, LF, nm $150, BER

Waterman

#452 sterling silver filigree, 1925, art nouveau
pattern, LF, nm $500, BER

Waterman

#5, 1926, LF, red ripple, red color band,
minimal wear but nm $150, GP

Waterman

452 Filigree, 1928, BHR LF, STSL overlay, fine $600, DN

Waterman

#0552 GF filigree, 1926, Gothic pattern,
LF, nm $450, BER

Waterman

452 STSL filigree, 1928, basket weave pattern,
LF, nm $450, BER

Waterman

41 Ripple, 1927, rare slender HR safety, 11.5 cm,
crisp and glossy, never inked, mint $650, DN

Waterman

752, 1925, BCHR LF, 13.6 cm, solid 14k gold trim,
clean pen, fine $250, DN

Waterman

452 1/2, 1926, sterling silver ringtop, working
condition, 14k nib $225, 1001

Waterman

Combination, 1927, LF, GFT, 14.2 cm,
fine $850, assorted sources

Waterman

752 1/2, 1920 BCHR, slender full-length LF,
GFT, fancy engraved barrel band, even
moderate fading, vg-fine $135, DN

Waterman
#54, 1924, BCHR, black $150, 1001

Waterman
Black hard rubber pen, 1906, 14k nib $250, 1001

United States Fountain Pen
*Victor, 1925, GF LF, 13.8 cm long, New York
made, fine parallel lines pattern, no dings,
fine quality* $270, DN

Unmarked
*Safety, 1925, clipless miniature, transparent pale
blue enamel over STSL with guilloche work,
cap crown marked "Sterling," "Germany,"
14k nib, exc* $500, DN

Unmarked
*Miniature ED, 1920, black hard rubber ringtop,
white casein cap crown, barrel marked
"Peggy Pen," vg* $65, DN

Unmarked
*Graf Zeppelin dip pen, 1930, .875 silver,
Estonian hallmarks, steel nib holder, will
not hold nibs, gd* $625, DN

Unmarked
*LF, 1930, fancy GF screw cap, initials
"JF" engraved on cap, no dents, 14k nib, nm* $220, DN

■

4

CONTENDERS FOR THE THRONE: THE 1930s

America at the end of World War I was on the brink of great prosperity. The Jazz Age spurred a new youthful spirit, a time when lavish lifestyles were cultivated, and corporation leaders in soaring towers of commerce such as the Woolworth and Wrigley buildings suddenly became the nation's heroes. President Calvin Coolidge (1923–1929) assured corporate leaders that "the business of America is business." It was perfectly acceptable for titans of industry to accumulate unfathomable wealth. Excess and exuberance was the ruling fashion, in keeping with the larger-than-life spirit of Harry Houdini, the sultanic Babe Ruth, and flappers, tipsy with gin, dancing the Charleston. Pens also became big and flamboyant, a mirror of the businessman's new affluence. No longer mere office items, they were suddenly transformed into fashion accessories, very portable signs of power and

Conklin All
American
Brown
Snakeskin
Plunger Filler
circa 1934

Sheaffer
Lifetime
Balance
circa 1934

sophistication. The 1920s and '30s are also known as
the pen's Gimmick Era, as all types of filling devices
were introduced and abandoned.

The **Parker Duofold** was certainly at the forefront of
the marketing phenomenon, produced by the company that created an undeniable buzz around pens.
Yet other manufacturers were writing their own success stories during this golden age, particularly in the
development of new materials, internal filling mechanisms, and ornamentation.

In this battle for supremacy, W. A. Sheaffer took the
lead in experimenting with celluloid, a very tough and
long-lasting plant fiber material that could be produced in a variety of colors. Recognizing that black

Eversharp
Equipoise,
Mid-1930s

Wahl-
Eversharp
Pacemaker Set
1938–1941

hard rubber pens had become outdated, this pioneer
of the lever fill system introduced a marbleized jade
green piece made of Dupont Radite (or pyroxalin
resin) in 1924 called the **Sheaffer Jade**. Mirroring the
jazzy spirit of the era, this dashing design was an immediate commercial success and soon a much-imi-
tated model for the entire industry. The Sheaffer Jade
was the first successful plastic pen. They are extremely durable, and non-discolored examples are
prized by collectors.

Sheaffer was previously known for its white-dotted
Lifetime pens and aniline-based **Skrip**, Sheaffer's
trade name for its fountain pen ink. The company refused to "merely" call it *ink*, claiming that it was better
than all other inks on the market, so Sheaffer marketed

Skrip as "the successor to ink." Sheaffer prospered from its **Radite** line until 1930. The country was then entering the Great Depression, following the stock market crash in October 1929, and in keeping with this leaner time of belt-tightening, Sheaffer moved away from large, cylindrical-shaped fountain pens and went streamlined with its hugely popular **Lifetime Balance** models. Radically distinct from blunt-ended pens of the past, the tapered Balance was offered in a range of attractive colors and remains a popular, smooth-writing collectible. Originally introduced with a lever filler, a redesigned **plunger-filled** Vac-Fil model triggered a costly advertising war with Parker, as both companies demanded credit for pioneering the first sac-less pen. Many of these $7 to $16 1930s Sheaffers with the characteristic white dot are difficult to find, yet available versions with inlaid abalone flakes or in red cherry are handsomely priced between $250 and $400. (The white dot appeared on Sheaffer's most expensive pens, signifying a lifetime warranty.)

Known for making **Eversharp** pencils during the Woodrow Wilson years (1913–1921), the Wahl company was another manufacturer of striking celluloid pens in the 1920s and '30s. Its most attractive offerings were the **Personal Point** (famed for a roller clip), the twelve-sided, art deco–inspired **Morocco Doric**, and the **Oxford**, with a 14-karat-gold point and the trademark double-checked medallion that was affixed to the company's most expensive pens.

Wahl subsequently introduced pens with a **safety ink shutoff** device that targeted the increasing number of airline passengers in the 1930s. Meant to be leakproof at high altitudes, these pens often failed miserably. But this marketing misstep was just the beginning of Wahl's problems. As Penoply's Rick Conner describes, this innovative manufacturer (later named Eversharp) became enmeshed in legal battles with ballpoint pen producers, and was devastated financially. Parker finally acquired the company in 1957, and although the **Skyline Demonstrator** was a beautiful 1990s attempt at resurrecting the brand, the Wahl-Eversharp legacy is best celebrated in its circa-1930s pieces.

Eversharp
Coronet Nib
Detail of
Safety Ink
Shutoff

Parker Royal
Challenger
and Deluxe
Challenger,
Late 1930s

Sheaffer
Balance
Oversize,
Mid-1930s

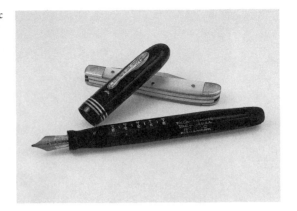

Conklin Nozac
Word Gauge
circa 1931

Conklin
Symetriks
from the Early
1930s

Adorned with attractive metal overlays, Conklin **crescent fillers** are another popular, reasonably priced collectible (those in scarcer red hard rubber are more expensive). Conklin never attained the dominance of Parker, Sheaffer, or Wahl-Eversharp, yet this U.S. manufacturer became distinguished for making America's only no-sac, or **Nozac**, **piston-filling** pen, in 1930. Marketed in a variety of styles and colors, round or polygonal, this signature item featured a **word gauge**, numbers indicating the number of words that could be written with the available ink supply. An $800 limited edition of the Nozac Word Gauge was released in 2000 (150 were produced), yet for those collectors insisting on historical accuracy, the stunning original model (along with Conklin's equally

Conklin Nozac
Pen Line circa
1935

Conklin
Symetrik circa
1931

attractive **Symetrik**) is surprisingly affordable, in the $400 range (see price list, p. 65).

Mabie Todd & Bard issued its first fountain pen, the **Calligraphic**, in 1878. The company introduced the **Swan** line between 1888 and 1889. According to David Moak's CD-ROM *Mabie in America*, 2nd Edition, "The choice of 'Swan' as the name for a pen model is entirely apt, as quills made from swan feathers were highly prized for their writing qualities, and 'pen' is also the word for a female swan." The company incorporated in 1907 and became Mabie, Todd & Co. It continued making pens, issuing the famous **Swan Leverless** (another gimmick) in the 1930s. Exquisite and featuring a **twist filling** mechanism (turning a knob enabled the sac to fill with ink), the celluloid,

Mabie Todd
Blackbird
from the Early
1930s

Mabie Todd
Swan Eternal
46 from the
Late 1920s

Mabie Todd
Leverless from
the Mid-1930s

easy-to-operate Leverless was offered in an array of silver and gold-filled overlays, and once the firm moved to England, the pen was advertised as "the pen of the British Empire."

Entering the highly competitive pen market in 1929, the German-based Pelikan company fashioned its own brand of reptile-patterned plastic pieces that continue to stir collectors' interest: the **Graphos,** which was used with waterproof inks. Punctuating this era of experimental filling mechanisms and colorful, intricately designed shapes and styles, there was Pelikan's still-popular **111T** or **Toledo**. An homage to the impeccable craftsmanship of Toledo sword makers, this art nouveau gem flaunted a specially engraved clip and a gold barrel sleeve with a pelican prominently displayed in the center. Extremely enticing, this Pelikan original might prove difficult to find, but there's also the recent re-creation, a limited edition beauty with a handcrafted vermeil sleeve overlaid with 24-karat gold. It too is an homage, to the inspired artistry of the 1930s.

Price List: 1930s

Because of the rich and diverse array of fountain pen models, the collector is confronted by a wide number of ink-fill systems and decorative features. It is therefore crucial to understand the abbreviations that are used on web sites and in retailers' catalogs.

These are the most common abbreviations:

- **BCHR**   Black Chased Hard Rubber
- **BF**   Button Filler
- **BHR**   Black Hard Rubber
- **CF**   Crescent Filler
- **CPT**   Chrome-Plated Trim
- **EXC**   Excellent Condition
- **GF**   Gold Filled
- **GFT**   Gold-Filled Trim
- **K**   Karat
- **LF**   Lever Filler
- **NM**   Near Mint Condition
- **PF**   Piston Filler

- **TF**   Twist Filler
- **VF**   Vacumatic Filler
- **VG**   Very Good Condition

The following price guide lists a sampling of pens produced by Parker and other major companies during the Jazz Age and years leading up to World War II. Brief pen descriptions are included along with the abbreviated names of the following reputable, well-established retailers who have at one point sold a particular pen (see "Pen Pals" in the Resource Guide for contact information). It must be noted that prices fluctuate, and it is best to contact the dealers for current market values.

- **DN**   David Nishimura Vintage Pens
- **EB**   eBay
- **FPH**   Fountain Pen Hospital
- **GP**   GoPens
- **JG**   Jim's Pen Site (Jim Gaston)
- **1001**   1001Pens
- **PB**   PenBox
- **PEH**   PenHero
- **PEN**   Penopoly
- **PH**   PenHome

Bayard
Excelsior fountain pen, 1941, brown marble $275, 1001

Bayard
La Suyserstyl #742 ladies, GFT Dulux, GFT band, mint $85, 1001

Big Ben
BF, 1938, orange, GFT, made in Denmark, fine $145, DN

Chameleon
Four Way, 1936, unusual in jade green double-nibbed combination, two-part barrel, inlaid color bands, vg-fine $450, DN

Chilton
Golden Quill, pneumatic fill, in burgundy, 1939, GFT, very rare model, Golden Quills come with GF inlaid teardrop-shaped indicia on back of cap, nm $400, GP

Chilton
*Wingflow, 1936, pneumatic filler, late bandless
pneumatic filler, unusual creamy green and
yellow marble with red veining, some
discoloration, vg-exc* $575, PH

Conklin
*Ink Visible No. 700, 1938, PF, lilac and
black celluloid, visible barrel, stub nib, mint
in box* $300, GP

Conklin
*Symetrik, plunger filler, 1934–38, fully restored,
translucent red stripe pattern, exc* $175, PEH

Conklin
Nozac, 1934, green marble $425, FPH

Conklin
#26, 1925, LF, BCHR, GFT, nm $125, GP

Conklin
*Endura Symetrik, 1937, rare, late Chicago-made
LF, 13 cm, GFT, greenish gray pearl and black,
internal linked pressure bar, crisp imprint,
fine-exc* $400, DN

Conklin
*"Halloween," #2 full size, 1927, black,
orange, and ivory swirl pattern, nm* $600, GP

Conklin
Endura, 1927, large sized, sapphire blue, nm $650, GP

Conklin
Endura, 1927, large sized, light jade, GFT, nm $550, GP

Conklin
*Endura Standard, 1927, black and bronze,
GFT, nm* $200, GP

Conklin
*#3 Lever, 1930, GF alternating wave with
plain panels* $175, GP

Conklin
*Nozac, 1933, red herringbone-patterned plastic,
visulated ink barrel, one of the few piston fillers
produced by American companies, exc* $400, PEN

Conklin
*Nozac Standard PIF, 1932, PF, 14-sided in green
pearl and black, GFT, exc* $300, GP

Conklin
*Endura, 1930, black and gold plastic, LF,
4-15/16", exc-nm* $375, PEN

Conklin
*Crescent filler, BCHR, fair amount of wear
to chasing on barrel, 5-3/8", vg* $275, PEN

Conklin
Nozac, gray striped, LF, 5-1/4" exc $150 PEN

Conklin
Ringtop CF, vg $175, PEN

Conway Stewart
#100 Duro, oversized in black, 14k nib, nm $465, 1001

Conway Stewart
#286, 1930–45, GFT clip and trim, LF $145, 1001

Conway Stewart
*Nippy No. 3, 1938, black, GFT, missing front
barrel band* $45, DN

Esterbrook
Dollar lever filler pen, 1939, copper, mint $50, GP

Eversharp
*Bantam, 1935, miniature bulb filler, 9.7 cm
gold plating worn on clip and steel nib,
good-vg* $45, DN

Eversharp
*Doric, TF, 4-9/16" long, adjustable nib with
shutoff valve, exc* $175, PEN

Eversharp
Doric, black plastic, 4 3/4, vg $125, PEN

Eversharp
*Doric pen and pencil set, silver herringbone,
TF, adjustable nib with ink shutoff, 5", exc* $375, PEN

John Dunhill
*Twopen, 1935, BHR two-nibbed pen, 14.6 cm long,
GFT, end knob turns to extend and retract
John Dunhill marked nibs, extremely clean
specimen of very rare and unusual pen, nm* $2,750, DN

Mabie, Todd & Co.
*Swan 330/00, leverless TF, 1934, russet and
jade, mint* $450, GP

Mabie, Todd & Co.
*#2 Blackbird, 1938, LF, in silver pearl, nm except
for plating wear* $75, GP

Mabie, Todd & Co.
#2 Blackbird, 1938, LF, in dark green, nm $95, GP

Mabie, Todd & Co.
*Blackbird, barrel band 2/60, 1938, black chased
celluloid, LF, 12.3 cm long, made in England,
usual age pitting to trim plating, fine* $110, DN

Mabie, Todd & Co.
142/52 LF, 1935, very attractive No. 2 Swan in
lapis blue, GF trim, vg-exc $258, PH

Mabie, Todd & Co.
Blackbird, 1935, LF, English made, Patrician-like
turquoise blue/gold, clipless model, exc $291, PH

Mabie, Todd & Co.
L212/88 FB, leverless, 1936, scarce No. 2 Swan
in emerald lizard, slight wear, no cracks $516, PH

Matcher
1930s, green marble BF, mint GFT band on
cap and trim snake clip, nm $165, 1001

Montblanc
432 Stylographic, 1937, black, PF, inlaid
white star on cap crown, GFT, ink window
transparency, vg-fine $300, DN

Montblanc
324, 1930s, BF, black, no cracks, no
scratches, vg $225, JG

Montblanc
326, 1935–36, black BF $225, JG

Montblanc
L139G, 1939, black celluloid plastic, largest
model of the company's top product
line, exc $2,000, PEN

Montblanc
326, 1936, BHR, rare large size of the
company's third-tier price line $450, PEN

Montblanc
322, BF pen and pencil set, 1930s, blue marbled,
"Luxury" model $1,200, JG

Moore
Lever filler, 1938, silver pearl marble, unusual
flat deco-style clip, fine-exc $80, DN

Omas
Extra Safety, 1932, very rare, GF octagonal
overlay with red and black enamel, 9.5 cm, no
dings or brassing, has not been recorked, exc $1,650, DN

Omas
Extra Lucens plunger filler, 1940, black with
GF trim, wartime nib $1,015, PH

Parker
Vacumatic Junior fountain pen and pencil set,
1938, gray marble, translucent barrel $175, GP

Parker
*Duofold Junior, 1933, lapis blue BF, 11.5 cm long,
GFT, feed and nib used but exc, perfect color,
crisp imprints, nm* $365, DN

Parker
Vacumatic Golden Web, 1936, VF, 4-3/4", vg $350, PEN

Parker
*Shadow Wave pen and pencil set, green striated,
1939, BF, 5-1/16", exc* $375, PEN

Parker
Vacumatic Demonstrator, vg $800, PEN

Parker
*Junior Vacumatic, 1935, unusual crystal
Vacumatic, clear, transparent barrel* $520, PH

Parker
*Vacumatic Imperial Debutante, 1938, brown
striated body with GF cap, Imperial models
(those with GF caps) are much less common
than regular Vacumatics, the smaller Debutante
size is rare, exc* $600, PEN

Parker
*Vacumatic filler, 1932, black junior size,
transparent barrel, 12.2 cm long, GFT, barrel
has darkened to ruby red, strong imprints,
fine longitudinal hairlines, fine-exc* $500, DN

Parker
*Vacumatic Junior, 1937, full-size Golden Web,
12.2 cm, lockdown filler, exc* $385, DN

Parker
*Premiere, 1934, blue pearl and black marble
BF, 12.4 cm fine-exc* $205, DN

Parker
*Duofold Geometric (toothbrush design) pen
and pencil set, 1939, brown marble and black,
BF, 5-1/16" vg* $350, PEN

Parker
*Royal Challenger, 1938, brown herringbone
plastic, 4-3/4", superb color, exc* $250, PEN

Parker
*Vacumatic, 1936, O/S, black, Vacumatic
filler, nm* $500, BER

Parker
*Challenger, 1939, gray pearl and black marble BF,
CPT, 13 cm, fine* $115, DN

Parker

*Vacumatic Junior, 1937, red pearl and black marble,
12.1 cm, GFT, lockdown filler, NM barrel transparency,
exc-nm* $225, DN

Parker

*Vacuum filler set in box, 1933, opaque black,
GFT, nice crisp imprints, unusual box with
reversible top, fine-exc* $650, DN

Parker

*Vacuum filler, 1933, silver pearl laminate, 12.9 cm,
white GFT, opaque barrel with integral section,
early form of arrow on two-tone nib, fine* $575, DN

Parker

*Vacumatic Junior, 1938, black Shadow wave,
12.4 cm, GFT, lockdown filler, nm barrel
transparency, fine* $205, DN

Parker

*Vacumatic Junior, 1938, black Shadow wave,
12.2 cm, GFT, lockdown filler, vg barrel
transparency, vg* $145, DN

Parker

*Vacumatic Debutante, 1938, small Shadow wave,
11.8 cm, unusual combination of gray with GF
instead of chrome trim, aluminum Speedline filler,
barrel transparency like new, mint* $275, DN

Parker

Challenger, 1935, green marble, BF, nm $100, BER

Parker

*Vacumatic, 1933–36, Oversize double gray stripe
jewel, 14k nib* $200, 1001

Parker

*Vacumatic, 1940, VF, large size, brown striated,
nm* $225, FPH

Parker

Standard Vacumatic, 1935, emerald pearl $235, PH

Parker

*Standard Vacumatic, 1935, golden web pattern,
good* $511, PH

Parker

Duofold, 1940, red and black marble $200, 1001

Parker

*Televisor Junior, 1935, green and black marbled,
GFT* £55, PB

Parker

*Duofold Senior, 1930s, marble desk base
complete with taper and original box* $310, PB

Pelikan
*100N, 1937, PF, in gray marble, rare model,
near mint* $200, GP

Pelikan
*100N, 1938, scarce black striated gray pearl,
HR cap and turning knob, good transparency,
strong imprints, exc* $550, DN

Pelikan
*100N PF, 1930, tortoise with red cap, blind cap with
turning knob, GFT, nm* $900, GP

Pelikan
*100CN PF, 1939, gray pearl, knurled turning
knob, GFT, nm* $300, GP

Pelikan
100N, 1939, in cobra color, nm $1,300, GP

Pelikan
100N, 1930, PF, gray marble, GFT, nm $450, GP

Pelikan
*Taylorix 100N PF, 1938, rare Taylorix in black, original 14k
nib, vg* $420, PH

Sheaffer
Model 5-30, 1933, LF, red-veined gray, GFT $100, GP

Sheaffer
*Feather Touch, 1936, LF, deep jade color,
GFT, nm* $100, GP

Sheaffer
*Lifetime Balance, 1937, full-sized LF, green striped,
nm* $350, GP

Sheaffer
*Balance, 1932, LF, red striated, feather-touch
balance, good condition* $225, PH

Sheaffer
*Balance Oversize Lifetime 1000, 1935, brown
pearl striated plunger filler, 13.9 cm long, GFT,
white dot, fine ink window transparency,
two-tone Lifetime nib* $450, DN

Sheaffer
*Balance Loaner, 1936, rare cherry red LF,
13.8 cm CPT, marked "Service Pen Loaned by
White Cross Pharmacy," fine-exc* $285, DN

Sheaffer
*Balance Oversize, 1933, red vein, silver and
gray marble, short hump clip, Lifetime nib,
LF exc-nm* $500, PEN

Sheaffer
Balance, 1932, brown stripe Radite plastic,
LF, nm $275, BER

Sheaffer
Balance Oversize, 1935, marine green
pearl, humped flat ball clip, exc $250, PEN

Sheaffer
Balance, black and pearl Radite, LF,
1932, nm $350, BER

Sheaffer
Balance Lifetime, 1941, large brown striated
military clip, plunger filler, white dot,
13.3 cm, exc barrel transparency, very clean pen,
fine-exc $120, DN

Sheaffer
Balance Oversize, 1000 pen and pencil set,
brown striped, LF, exc $350, PEN

Wahl-Eversharp
Oversize Equipoise, 1936, bronze and green LF,
GFT, 13.8 cm, military roller clip, beautiful
color, minimal wear, exc-nm $850, DN

Wahl-Eversharp
Equipoise, 1936, jade green LF, 13.8 cm, military
roller clip, GFT, moderate discoloration,
fine-exc $450, DN

Wahl-Eversharp
Ladies pen, 1929, LF with gold overlay, missing
nib, £68, PB

Wahl-Eversharp
Lever filler, rippled red hard rubber, military
clip, exc $200, PEN

Wahl-Eversharp
Gold Seal, 1936, nacre black and pearl plastic.
Oversize model is greatly desired; the nacre color
was susceptible to intense ambering (darkening).
This model is unusual because the discoloring
is not extreme, vg $600, PEN

Wahl-Eversharp
Doric, 1938, cashmere (green marble plastic).
Oversize model is greatly desired and not
common, exc $800, PEN

Wahl-Eversharp
Doric, 1938, jet (black) plastic. Oversize
model is greatly desired and not
common, exc $800, PEN

Wahl-Eversharp
Doric Oversize Silver Seal, 1931, LF, smoked gray color is rare, adjustable nib $650, GP

Wahl-Eversharp
Signature set in box, 1929, full-size Gold Seal black and pearl LF, 13.4 cm GFT, pencil uses 1.1 mm lead, clean set, box worn, smooth nib $395, DN

Wahl-Eversharp
Oversize Equipoise, 1932, black LF, 14.5 cm, GFT, vg $550, DN

Wahl-Eversharp
Doric Gold Seal Oversize, 1931–34, LF, 5 3/14", exc $1,075, PEN

Wahl-Oxford
Lever filler in green bronze marble, 5-3/8", beautiful color, good $120, PEN

Waterman
#94, 1930, LF, brown cream, GFT, nm $250, GP

Waterman
Ink View Deluxe, 1935, LF, black, nm $350, GP

Waterman
#2, 1939, LF, smooth sterling silver, rare streamlined model, rare, nm $500, GP

Waterman
Patrician, 1935, onyx plastic, LF, nm $1,200, BER

Waterman
754, 1938, BCHR LF, 13.6 cm, 14k solid gold trim, includes Odd Fellows emblem on cap, matte finish, chasing clean but barrel number absent, fine-exc $285, DN

Waterman
403, 1938, late silver filigree LF, scratches on cap overlay, fine-exc $600, DN

Waterman
Gregg, 1935, black LF, GFT, enamel emblem at cap top, "Gregg" stamped on clip, made for Gregg shorthand, fine $250, DN

Waterman
52V Persian, 1930, LF ringtop, GFT, scarce, fine-exc $300, DN

Waterman
Combination, 1930, rare uncataloged model, black and pearl LF, CPT, vg-fine $1,100, DN

Waterman
*94 Ripple, 1930, olive ripple HR, GFT, 12.8 cm
imprint weak, clip slightly bent, hairline above
clip, mechanically sound and handsome,
good-vg* $275, DN

Waterman
*Ink View Deluxe Set LF, 1935, Emerald Ray, Waterman's
answer to the Parker Vacumatic with a pump-filling
mechanism and a translucent barrel, nm* $700, GP

Waterman
*Ink View Standard LF Demonstrator, 1935, rare
one-piece lever bar, bottom of barrel
engraved, nm* $425, GP

Wyvern
*Perfect pen No. 81, 1939, copper pearl marble,
LF, 13.1 cm long, GFT, sealed cap lip hairline, vg* $90, DN

◼

5

A WORLD OF CHANGE: 1940–1970

Shaped by World War II, the growing struggle for civil rights, the rise of communism, and the cold war, the frenetic 1940s and '50s meant sweeping cultural changes. Women were leaving home to join the workplace while millions of men were in uniform, and in the spirit of this Great Emancipation, African Americans, led by the pioneering Jackie Robinson—the first African American player to break the "color line" in professional baseball—also demanded new freedoms. All Americans, once World War II ended, hoped to enjoy greater leisure time and a return to peacetime prosperity the nation had not known since before the stock market crash of 1929. But even with the coming of television, the baby boom, and big-band music, this period of great social revolution also brought profound disillusionment. As the clouds

Waterman
Dauntless
Blue Marble
and Black
Commando,
Late 1940s

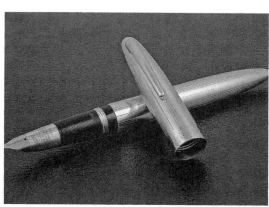

Sheaffer Solid
Gold
Masterpiece,
Late 1940s

Parker 51
Signet
Aerometric
Set circa 1949

over Nagasaki and Hiroshima lingered, Americans entered the atomic age.

Early on during these years, pen manufacturers were hard-pressed to find various materials and were forced to reengineer their designs. Such strategic wartime materials as brass, steel, and aluminum were in short supply during the 1940s, and this meant greater usage of gold and silver. Celluloid still gave manufacturers the freedom to offer a variety of patterns and colors, but during the war, America had experienced its first taste of food rationing and consumer goods shortages.

The postwar years were a new era, a time to re-create, repackage, and reinvent pens to meet the challenges posed by the rise of labor unions, the scarcity of traditional materials, and the advent of plastics. The future was *now*, and to get into step with the space age fostered by airplane travel, automobiles with big-finned taillights, and the sudden prominence of scientists, pens were flamboyantly marketed as streamlined, jet-styled, torpedoes, and missile-like. They had to be invested with this cutting-edge technology, because looming on the horizon was an invention that would ultimately devastate the fountain pen industry.

Clearly influenced by World War II's military lexicon, Mabie, Todd & Company introduced the **Torpedo**, a celluloid pen with gold-plated clips, in 1948. The Torpedo was filled by twisting the end of the barrel— which proved to be inefficient—and was offered in five colors: Morocco (a reddish-brown marble), Cathay, Burma, Jet, and Kashmir.

Trying to stay competitive, Sheaffer offered the simple-to-use, two-tone **Touchdown** series with chrome caps, plastic barrels, and gold-filled clips in 1949. This elegant series, which continues to stir enthusiasm among aficionados, featured the **Admiral**, **Valiant**, and **Sovereign** models—pneumatic-filling pens that enjoyed smooth sailing in the marketplace well into the 1950s.

Turning to the seas for inspiration, Sheaffer issued its **Snorkel** line in 1952. Resembling the spy-craft paraphernalia engineered by Q in a James Bond film, the

Parker Duofolds, 1940s, a Vacumatic and a Button Filler

Esterbrook Desk Pen, Late 1940s

Snorkel with its array of sacs, tubing, and filler springs has been described by David Nishimura as "the most mechanically complex pen ever produced." Ambitiously fashioning a pen that didn't have to be dipped into ink, in 1959 Sheaffer offered the more macho **PFM** (Pen for Men) **Snorkels**, oversized **Masterpiece** and **Clipper** versions with 14-karat-gold nibs and gold-filled bands. A commercial failure, these self-fillers in dark blue, burgundy, and green were manufactured only in small quantities, resulting in a scarcity that makes them ideal to collect.

As Nishimura points out, "The [letters] 'PFM' do not appear anywhere on a PFM, which has led to some confusion among the inexperienced. All PFMs are self-fillers with a snorkel-filling tube. The smaller Sheaffer

Sheaffer
Snorkel
Valiant,
1952–1959

Sheaffer
Touchdown
Valiant,
1949–1950

Imperial, produced in both **Touchdown** and cartridge versions, is worth only a fraction of a PFM." The PFM is a large pen, and these have gained new popularity among collectors.

Even more attractive for new enthusiasts with a limited budget, **Esterbrook** single or double jewel **J** pens—old-fashioned, lever fillers in either solid, marbled, or pastel colors—were a low-priced favorite among students in the 1940s and '50s. These pens did not have actual jewels in them, but plastic end pieces. A mix of celluloid, steel points, and nickel-plated accents, the easily found Js won't ever bring stratospheric investment returns, but they write well, and are a well-built, good-looking choice for starting a

Sheaffer PFM
III, 1959–1968

Esterbrook
Copper J,
Late 1940s

collection. J pens from Esterbrook's deluxe chrome-capped series are more difficult to find.

Another 1940s favorite, Eversharp took the unprecedented step of employing industrial designers to style futuristic-looking pens. The "father" of the Electrolux vacuum, Raymond Loewy, put his distinctive touches on the streamlined **Symphony**, and Henry Dreyfuss incorporated aesthetic elements of his 20th Century Limited locomotive into the **Skyline** pen. This pen, with gold-filled or solid gold trim, has become extremely popular with collectors—even though the plastic was inferior and often cracks—and points to a time when Eversharp was in the same lofty realm as Parker and Sheaffer.

Eversharp
Skylines,
Including an
Uncommon
Chevron
Pattern Pen,
1941–1948

Eversharp
Skyline Black
circa 1942

Eversharp
Symphony
1948

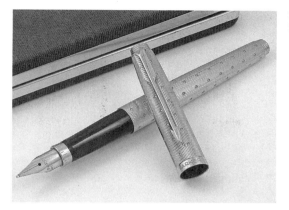

Parker 75
Perle circa
1968

Parker 45
Convertible,
Early 1960s

The 1940s were also the time of the Great Comeback. Once the bombs stopped falling over Germany, the Simplo Filler Company that had long made distinguished safety and eyedropper pens could resume production (the factory had been destroyed), and market its soon-to-be prized **Meisterstück** or **Masterpiece** edition. It would take several years before Simplo, or later Montblanc (the white top of the cap is supposed to suggest the snow-covered Swiss Alps mountain) became idealized as icons of luxury, renowned for such investment-quality limited editions as the **Hemingway** and **Lorenzo de Medici,** with the 4,810 numerals representing the height of the mountain engraved on the cap and nib. Montblanc's resurrection of immortal writers (with **Marcel**

Proust, **Mozart**, and **Agatha Christie** pens) would soar to very high prices, and the very fat, jet black **149 Masterpiece** (made after 1952) retains its original allure. More strongly built than its injection-molded predecessors, this hefty classic is the stuff of legend, and is still reasonably priced.

After suspending production during World War II, Pelikan restyled its line with a pen that featured a clip shaped like a pelican's beak. In 1959 it offered a more streamlined American-looking **piston filler** called the **P1**. Pelikan's commercial efforts and other companies' technological advancements still failed to weaken Parker's hold on the market with its easily filled 51s and 61s. Yet the "magic" of these capillary fillers often proved to be illusory, and their inefficiency led to Parker's use of a **cartridge converter system** by the 1960s.

The unreliability of many fountain pens is a recurring theme during this era. As post–World War II consumers became more leisure-time oriented, they grew tired of expensive, "old-fashioned" writing instruments requiring elaborate mechanisms, refillings, and maintenance. They wanted jet-age simplicity, the ultimate in streamlined "no fuss, no bother" mechanics. But consumers were never actually offered the "perfect" ballpoint in the mid-1940s. They were instead made to wait while pen makers waged numerous legal squabbles and patent wars.

Price List: Circa 1940–1960s

Because of the rich and diverse array of fountain pen models, the collector is confronted by a wide number of ink-fill systems and decorative features. It is therefore crucial to understand the abbreviations that are used on web sites and in retailers' catalogs.

These are the most common abbreviations:

- **AF**   Aerometric Filler
- **BF**   Button Filler
- **EXC**   Excellent Condition
- **GD**   Good Condition
- **GF**   Gold Filled

- **GFT**   Gold-Filled Trim
- **K**   Karat
- **LF**   Lever Filler
- **NM**   Near Mint Condition
- **PF**   Piston Filler
- **PL**   Pump Lever
- **STSL**   Sterling Silver
- **VF**   Vacumatic Filler
- **VG**   Very Good Condition

The following price guide mainly lists a sampling of pens produced during the 1940s and '50s. Brief pen descriptions are included, along with the abbreviated names of the reputable, well-established retailers who have at one point sold a particular pen (see "Pen Pals," in the Resource Guide, for contact information). It must be noted that prices fluctuate, and it is best to contact the dealers for current market values.

- **BER**   Berliner Pens
- **DN**   David Nishimura Vintage Pens
- **EB**   eBay
- **FPH**   Fountain Pen Hospital
- **GP**   GoPens
- **JG**   Jim's Pen Site
- **1001**   1001Pens
- **PB**   PenBox
- **PEH**   PenHero
- **PEN**   Penopoly
- **PH**   PenHome

Aurora
88, 1949, "585" nib, exc   *$180, EB*

Conway Stewart
#22, 1955, LF, floral design on yellow background,
14k gold nib, mint   *$1,030, 1001*

Conway Stewart
Uncommon tiger's eye LF, 1950, English   *$322, PH*

Conway Stewart
#27, GFT wide band on cap, LF in silver gray,
hatched design, mint   *$265, 1001*

Conway Stewart
#60, 1950, green herringbone pattern,
original box $410, 1001

Conway Stewart
#84, red and gold veins, 1952–63, LF,
near mint $100, 1001

Conway Stewart
#75 in black, 1952, GFT clip $95, 1001

Conway Stewart
#84 in black, 1952–63, LF, GF clip and trim $95, 1001

Conway Stewart
#75 in blue marble, 1952, extra fine, 14k nib $100, 1001

Conway Stewart
#15, 1950, black-veined blue pearl, LF,
12.8 cm long, hairline on edge of clip
screw, exc $120, DN

Conway Stewart
Model 24 LF, 1951, marine pearl hatched
(lavender web), rare color, GFT, mint in box $275, GP

Conway Stewart
#15, 1955, black LF, 12.8 cm, GFT, cap bands
slightly loose, mint $165, DN

Conway Stewart
27, 1955, LF, green candy stripe, broad single
cap band, vg-exc $233, PH

Conway Stewart
100 Duro, 1955, large No. 100 in black, top
condition $407, PH

Conway Stewart
Dinkie 570, 1960, one of the last Dinkies in
translucent blue, exc $123, PH

Esterbrook
No. 2140, 1960, desk set in box, round ceramic
base and matching LF in lime, pen has clear
top, mint $160, DN

Esterbrook
Pink pastel, 1950, LF, mint $75, GP

Esterbrook
Green pen with black vertical striping, 1955,
rare, mint $75, GP

Esterbrook
Ladies purse pen, circa 1950s, yellow $120, EB

Esterbrook
Blue pearlized, 5" long, #2968 nib, minimal
wear $16, EB

Esterbrook
Red pearl laminate, 1950s, PL filler, exc $16, EB

Esterbrook
SJ, black, needs new sac, otherwise exc $10, EB

Esterbrook
Silver pearl, mint $15, EB

Esterbrook
Dubonnet red, 1944–47, 3-ribbed cap button,
restored, exc $50, JG

Eversharp
Skyline, 1943, black LF, 13.2 cm, GFT, less
common variant with clip that doesn't extend
over cap crown, barrel slightly bent, nm $95, DN

Eversharp
Skyline, 1941–49, dove gray, LF, restored,
vg-exc $95, JG

Eversharp
Skyline, 1945, black LF, scarce and attractive,
GF cap with engine turning, fine-exc $175, DN

Eversharp
Skyline navy, 1943–49, celluloid cap, navy barrel
and derby, 5-1/4", less common wide band,
cap has small dings, gd $35, PEH

Eversharp
Slim Ventura gray, 1953–57, AF, GF cap and
gray plastic barrel, 5-1/8", minimal scuffing
on barrel $35, PEH

Eversharp
Skyline black, 1943–49, cap and barrel minimal
scuffing, gd $40, PEH

Eversharp
Symphony, 1950, black LF, 14 cm gold-plated
cap, minor shop wear, nm $90, DN

Eversharp
Skyline, 1941–49, forest green, 14k nib, vg $96, JG

Eversharp
Ventura, 1954–57, STSL, 14k nib, AF, no
dings, exc $225, JG

Mabie, Todd & Co.
Blackbird 5277, 1948, LF, unused bandless
Blackbird in bright red, GF clip, top condition $155, PH

Montblanc
25 Meisterstück (Masterpiece), 1941, push-knob
filler, 12-sided model in green marble, nm $1,250, GP

Montblanc

246 PIF, PF, 1946, light green, black veins,
large pen, nm $775, GP

Montblanc

134 PIF, 1947, PF, black, nm $450, GP

Montblanc

146G PIF, 1950, green stripe, rare, largest pen
MB made in this beautiful celluloid, nm $1,250, GP

Montblanc

342 PIF in gray, 1955, GFT, visulated barrel,
minor scuffs $225, GP

Montblanc

042 MonteRosa PIF, 1957, in green, very
rare color, GFT, visulated barrel, nm $150, GP

Montblanc

149 Masterpiece PIF in black, 1959, early
version with STSL outer bands, GFT, nm $850, GP

Montblanc

Meisterstück 742 PF, 1952, GF model, no
dents, no imprints, 14k nib, vg $550, JG

Montblanc

246 Piston, 1946, light green marble, large
ink window $765, PH

Montblanc

138 Meisterstück PIF in black, 1945, two-tone
medium nib, one of the largest MB pens of the
era, quite rare, long barrel window, GFT, nm $1,500, GP

Montblanc

246, 1948, green marble plastic, produced in
company's Danish factory, largest size in
product line, exc $500, PEN

Montblanc

744N, 1957, GF metal, uncommon all GF
model, exc $650, PEN

Montblanc

642 PIF in silver stripe, 1950, brushed stainless
steel cap, beautifully offset with GF clip and
cap band, nm $725, GP

Montblanc

212 BF in black, 1955, GFT, nm $245, GP

Montblanc

146G PIF, 1950, PF, black with silver stripe,
nm $1,300, GP

Montblanc

144 Demonstrator, 1952, rare, nm $300, GP

Montblanc
139 PIF, 1952, PF, black celluloid, STSL
outer cap bands, near mint $2,000, GP

Parker
Blue Diamond Major, 1945, Vacumatic,
black with semi-transparent barrel,
original box $205, PEN

Parker
Duofold Senior, 1941, streamline BF, bronze
pearl-lined web pattern, English made, rare
and beautiful, nm $550, GP

Parker
51 Redband, 1946, black with Lustraloy cap,
unique filling briefly manufactured by Parker
and later recalled, mint $850, PEN

Parker
Challenger, 1941–45, black plastic, fine $85, 1001

Parker
Duofold Senior, 1940, red and gray pearl with
black stripes, Blue Diamond clip, triple-cap
band, aluminum Speedline filler, 13.4 cm,
largest size, blind cap trim ring missing, vg $175, DN

Parker
Duofold, 1941, VF, red and gray pearl with
black stripes, GFT, double jewel, 13.1 cm,
near mint transparency, Speedline filler,
scratch on wide patterned cap band, fine-exc $180, DN

Parker
51, 1946, royal blue with Lustraloy cap,
Prototype color never released to the public,
VF, nm $5,000, PEN

Parker
51, 1941, gray with sterling silver wedding band
cap, first-year models are uncommon, Parker 51
on blind cap rather than on top of barrel as
on later production years, aluminum jewels on
top of cap and bottom of barrel are unique
to first-year models, exc $550, PEN

Parker
51, 1948, black barrel/GF cap, VF, nm $150, BER

Parker
Oversize Vacumatic, 1940, red laminated,
GFT, some wear $450, GP

Parker
Vacumatic Golden Pearl, 1947, VF, nm $100, BER

Parker
Vacumatic, 1948, gray, 14k nib, restored, VF, exc $95, JG

Parker
45 Custom Turquoise, 1968, early aerometric-type
squeeze bar, GF trim, converter included,
vg-exc $30, PEH

Parker
61, 1961–69, has not been inked, original box
and price tag, mint $165, PEH

Parker
51 Vacumatic, 1947, cordovan brown, unusual
style, Blue Diamond, Vac filler, restored, exc $135, JG

Parker
Vacumatic, black laminate barrel, VF, 14k nib,
restored, vg-exc $105.50, JG

Parker
Vacumatic Standard, 1944, blue laminated,
GFT, nm $100, GP

Parker
51 Vacumatic, 1946, in black, brushed Lustraloy
(stainless steel) cap, GF clip, nm $75, GP

Parker
51 Aerometric, 1952, burgundy, silver cap,
stub nib, nm $195, GP

Parker
51 Aerometric, 1950, dark blue, GF cap $175, GP

Parker
Blue Diamond Major Vacumatic, 1945, in
blue pearl, semi-transparent barrel, vg $240, PH

Parker
51 Aerometric, 1950, black, GF cap, mint
in box $200, GP

Parker
45 Coronet, 1960, cartridge/converter, mint
in box $150, GP

Parker
45 Signet, 1960, cartridge/converter,
14k nib, nm $75, GP

Parker
51 Demi, 1947, in gray, lined GF cap, exc $344, PH

Parker
45, 1970, cartridge/converter, dark gray, mint
in box $125, GP

Parker
45 Coronet, 1970, cartridge/converter, black
anodized metal, nm $125, GP

Parker
T-1, 1970, cartridge converter, titanium, mint $700, GP

Parker
Vacumatic Junior, 1942, red, silver, and black
vertical striped, GFT, nm $90, GP

Parker
Vacumatic Major, 1941, scarce blue pearl laminate
double jewel, 13.4 cm, GFT, Blue Diamond clip,
vg barrel transparency, fine-exc $285, DN

Parker
Vacumatic Maxima, 1941, brown pearl laminate Oversize
double jewel, 13.3 cm, GFT, Blue Diamond clip, aluminum
Speedline filler, black section and jewels, exc transparency,
two-tone nib, fine $405, DN

Parker
51, 1942, black double jewel, unmarked silver cap
with rare grouped parallel lines pattern, two-tone
clutch ring, very unusual pen from beginning of
wartime production, fine $625, DN

Parker
51 set in box, 1945, buckskin tan double jewel, rare
"Empire" two-tone 14k solid gold caps and trim,
Blue Diamond clip, two-tone clutch ring, exc
evenness of color, caps crisp, nm $2,500, DN

Parker
51, 1946, tan double jewel, unusual cap with alternating
straight and squiggly lines, Blue Diamond clip,
minimal wear to cap, exc $500, DN

Parker
51, 1946, dark blue Vac filler, unusual Lustraloy cap,
wide raised band with fine parallel lines, Blue
Diamond clip, vg-fine $150, DN

Parker
Vacumatic Major, 1945, brown pearl laminate,
12.8 cm, Blue Diamond clip, good transparency,
wartime cap band is GF over silver, g-vg $90, DN

Parker
51, 1946, mustard double jewel, gold-filled cap
with grouped parallel lines, Blue Diamond clip,
14k solid gold tassie, initials "J.C.B." on barrel,
slight indentations on cap, beautifully even
color, exc $500, DN

Parker
51, 1946, black double jewel with scarce grid pattern,
GF "Heirloom" cap, 14k solid gold trim, Blue
Diamond clip, exc-nm $685, DN

Parker
*51 Demi, 1947, gray Vac filler, Lustraloy cap,
exc-nm* $165, DN

Parker
*51 Demi Signet, 1948, unusual short AF, 12.9 cm
long, GF cap and barrel, grouped parallel lines
pattern, no dings, filler marked "Press . . .
6 Times," exc-nm* $650, DN

Parker
*51 Demi, 1948, cocoa AF, frosty Lustraloy
cap, sac transparency exc, nm* $185, DN

Parker
*51 Demi set in box, 1950, black AF and injector
pencil, frosty Lustraloy cap, like new, barely
used, nm* $275, DN

Parker
*51, 1954, cocoa AF, frosty Lustraloy cap, has
not been filled, mint* $250, DN

Parker
*51, 1956, dark blue AF, frosty Lustraloy cap,
perfect sac transparency, mint* $225, DN

Parker
*51 Presidential, 1965, in 9k gold, wavy-like
decoration, 14k nib, nm* $1,747, PB

Parker
Vacumatic Imperial, exc $700, PEN

Parker
*105 fountain pen and ballpoint set, 1970, GF,
no scratches* $340, PB

Parker
Duofold AF, 1948, aluminum BF $126, PB

Parker
*61 Presidential, 9k, 1966, teardrop design,
cartridge/converter, minimal wear* $942, PB

Parker
*Victory MK4, 1948, aluminum BF in dark
brown* $87, PB

Parker
*51 Blue Diamond Clip, 1946, navy blue,
14k nib* $155, 1001

Parker
*65 Consort Insignia, 1969, heavy rolled gold
cap and barrel, pearlized jewels to cap and
barrel, mint* $382, PB

Parker
17, 1957–62, cartridge, black $88, 1001

Parker
Duofold Senior, 1958, red, fine $175, 1001

Parker
*VS, 1947, red brown BF, Lustraloy cap, clear Lucite
feed, vg* $90, DN

Parker
*Victory Mark IV, 1949, black GFT, 2nd GFT, 13.2 cm,
made in England, vg* $140, assorted sources

Parker
*Popular, 1950, black BF, GFT, made in Denmark,
exc-mint* $175, DN

Parker
*21, 1956, AF, frosty Lustraloy cap with polished
rim, nm sac transparency, nm* $70, DN

Parker
*Signet, 1963, GF cap and band, capillary filler,
nm* $265, DN

Parker
*61, circa 1957–62, capillary filler, GFT cap,
mint* $175, 1001

Parker
51 Blue Diamond clip, 1946, Vacumatic filler $150, 1001

Parker
65 Flighter, AF $145, 1001

Parker
Duofold, ladies striped, 1940–45, red, 14k nib $95, 1001

Parker
T-1, 1970, converter, titanium, matte gray $1,035, PH

Parker
51 Arrow Clip, 1952, AF, GFT clip, 14k point $175, 1001

Parker
61, 1957, self-filler $90, 1001

Parker
T-1, 1970, cartridge/converter, nm barrel $650, FPH

Parker
*51, AF, circa mid-1950s, GF cap, black, burgundy,
and gray bands, mint* $225, FPH

Parker
51, 1953, AF, GF cap, black, burgundy, gray $195, FPH

Parker
17 Super, 1964, AF, green $115, PH

Parker
*17, circa 1950s, hooded nib, in various colors such as
burgundy, black* $95 to $125, EB

Parker
61, 1964, capillary filler, red, heirloom cap, unused,
exc $235, PH

Parker
61, Consort Insignia, 1965, gold design on cap
and barrel $375, PH

Parker
21 Super, 1964, AF, brushed stainless cap, Arrow clip, exc sac
transparency, exc-nm $65, DN

Parker
61 Flighter, 1968, stainless steel cap and body, cartridge or
converter filler, made in England, exc-nm $265, DN

Parker
Slimfold, 1965, blue English-made AF, 12.6 cm long, exc sac
transparency, GFT, exc-nm $80, DN

Parker
T-1, 1970 (pen made only this year), includes converter,
brushed titanium, mint $985, DN

Parker
61, rainbow cap, aqua band, alternating yellow and pink
gold, exc $120, EB

Parker
51 desk pen, 1970, AF, exc $45, JG

Parker
UK Victory model, 1960s, forest green, vg to exc "Bullet
Proof" AF $90, JG

Parker
Flighter, 1960, stainless steel, capillary action
filler, nm $225, BER

Parker
51, 1960, AF, satin finish, Lustraloy cap, black,
exc $223, PB

Parker
45, 1970, black/stainless, cartridge or converter
fill $460, BER

Parker
75, 1965, converter, early 75 in vermeil, flat tassies,
exc $210, PH

Parker
51 AF, 1960, GF custom 51 in forest green,
top condition $507, PH

Pelikan
100N, 1947–51, PF, two-tone green, decorated
clip, vg $350, JG

Pelikan
112, 1942, PF, pinstripe with alternating panels, 14k gold
overlay, nm $1,500, GP

Pelikan
400 NN, 1956–63, brown tortoise motif, orig.
nib, good $102, EB

Pelikan
400 NN, 1955, light tortoise/gray striped celluloid,
PF, nm $140, EB

Pelikan
100 NN, 1949–54, green marbled band, black cap,
fluting along length, 14k nib, filling system works
perfectly $95, EB

Pelikan
500 PF, 1950, translucent green with black stripes
and pinstriped GF cap, rare, nm $500, GP

Sheaffer
Triumph Crest 1500, 1946, black LF, 13.1 cm, crisp
GF cap and trim, white dot on barrel end,
visulated section, like new, two-tone conical
Triumph nib, exc-nm $145, DN

Sheaffer
PFM IV, 1960, burgundy, chrome cap, GFT,
white dot, fine-exc $385, DN

Sheaffer
Statesman Snorkel, 1955, black GF trim,
lifetime white dot model, vg $140, PH

Sheaffer
Snorkel, GF $134, EB

Sheaffer
Statesman, lifetime white dot model, 1955,
Snorkel filler, black, GFT $140, PH

Sheaffer
Clipper Snorkel, 1950s white dot cap, Snorkel
filler, palladium silver nib, restored, exc $105, JG

Sheaffer
Valiant, 1955, Snorkel Touchdown filler, gray,
GF cap, mint $225, PH

Sheaffer
PFM III, 1964, Snorkel Touchdown filler in
black, gd $225, PH

Sheaffer
Imperial, plunger, 1970, Touchdown filler, exc $245, EB

Sheaffer
PFM V Snorkel in black, 1959, GFT, mint in
original box $325, GP

Sheaffer
Lifetime Triumph Touchdown filler, 1950,
GF pinstripe, nm $125, GP

Sheaffer
PFM V, 1961, black with GF cap,
Snorkel fill, nm $375, BER

Sheaffer
PFM III, burgundy plastic, Snorkel fill, 1961, nm $275, BER

Sheaffer
PFM I, black plastic, Snorkel fill, 1961, nm $175, BER

Sheaffer
Snorkel Statesman, 1955–59, buckskin tan,
uncommon color, 5 1/2" capped, palladium/
silver Triumph nib, no visible brassing $125, PEH

Sheaffer
PFM III Snorkel, 1959, burgundy, nm $175, GP

Sheaffer
PFM III Touchdown Snorkel, 1964, in black, vg $265, PH

Sheaffer
Imperial plunger, 1970, STSL Touchdown
filler, exc-nm $245, PH

Sheaffer
PFM Snorkel, 1959, gray, GF pinstripe cap,
a few dings in cap crown, otherwise nm $400, GP

Wahl-Eversharp
Skyline, 1944, solid 14k cap and barrel, LF $600, BER

Wahl-Eversharp
Pen and pencil set, 1944, 14k cap, black
barrel, LF, nm $400, BER

Wahl-Eversharp
Skyline Junior fountain pen and pencil in
burgundy, GF cap, 1943, gd $75, GP

Waterman
Commando "Cleric," 1942, LF, black, rare
model, mint $145, GP

Waterman
#2 LF in black, 1945, relatively late, simple pen,
GFT, nm $65, GP

Waterman
Cartridge pen, 1949, GFT cap, 18k nib $175, 1001

Waterman
Cartridge pen, 1949, GFT clip, pen and box $150, 1001

Waterman
W5 pen and pencil set, 1955, LF, one of the
largest Watermans in 1950s, original box and
instructions, exc $226, PH

Waterman
Cartridge pen, 1949, GF clip $250, 1001

Waterman
Lever filler, black, GFT, identical to Commando
model, fine $75, EB

Waterman
Taperite set, 1948, solid 14k gold, 13.7 cm LF,
pencil uses .9 mm lead, vg $680, DN

Waterman
Stateleigh Taperite, 1948, black LF, semi-hooded
nib, GF Hundred Year–style cap, exc-nm $125, DN

Waterman
Cartridge fountain pens, 1955, dealer package of
12 individually boxed chrome-capped pens with
semi-hooded steel nibs in assorted colors, spare
cartridges and instructions included, mint $500, DN

Waterman
Crusader, 1946–49, gray, 14k nib, vg imprints,
sac is pliable $25, PEH

■

6

THE BALLPOINT PEN

Long before the "pen wars" erupted in the 1940s, an obscure leather worker perfected an instrument that was to radically alter the course of writing history. His name was John J. Loud, and although his efforts never attracted the attention of anyone like Baron Bich, Laszlo Biro, Space Pen impresario Paul Fisher, or others who would become famous in the development of ballpoint pens, this tanner-turned-inventor still overcame "the impossible."

Unable to mark his hides with a fountain pen, Loud experimented with numerous substances, trying to find an ink that would not smudge and skip. Despite his tannery's uninviting conditions, where all sorts of chemicals and liquids complicated the development of smooth-working inks, Loud persevered and finally patented a ballpoint pen in 1888.

Featuring a rotating ball that was held in a socket, and relying on gravity to allow a supply of heavy ink to flow

Sheaffer
Stratowriter,
Eversharp CA,
and CA
Retractable
circa 1946

toward the point, Loud's quick-drying pen was the model for the modern ballpoint. Yet even though Loud can arguably be called the father of this revolutionary writing tool, his pen attracted little commercial interest, and little is known about the man himself.

Other would-be inventors tried to devise their own leak- and smudge-free pens, but it was not until 1938 that a pair of Hungarian brothers introduced the first ballpoint. A journalist, sculptor, and medical student who invented an automatic automobile gearbox, Laszlo Biro (1899–1985) grew increasingly dissatisfied with inks that didn't dry quickly enough or flowed too freely and smudged his work. Collaborating with his brother Georg, a chemist, he ultimately designed the **Biro** (1938), a ballpoint containing a rotating tungsten ball bearing at the tip and a brass socket that again depended on gravity to ensure a continuous flow of pigmented, gelatin-based ink. Fleeing war-torn Europe, the Biro brothers immigrated to Argentina and patented their newly developed device. They soon sold the Biro's marketing rights to Eterpen, which in turn supplied the British Royal Air Force with pens that purportedly wouldn't leak at high altitudes.

The aviation age was dawning, and once the tubular, modern-looking Biro was promotionally linked to those heroic "flyboys," this pen became synonymous with cutting-edge technology. It did so well that the Eversharp Company partnered with Eberhard-Faber to purchase the Biro's marketing and production rights from Eterpen in 1945. The capillary action Biro was then rechristened the **Eversharp CA**.

The Biro/CA also attracted the attention of a flamboyant stock market speculator who imported cigarette lighters into the United States during World War II and had accumulated a new fortune after recouping from three bankruptcies. Visiting Argentina in early 1945, Chicago businessman Milton Reynolds was so enthralled by the Biro that he researched patent laws and soon produced his own $12.50 **Rocket** ballpoint. When the Reynolds Rocket was introduced in October 1945, at Gimbel's department store in New York, it was priced at $12.50 and 8,000 units were sold on the first day. This was a very high price for a new and essentially unproven pen, but the public was excited and bought all they could get.

Before Eversharp could introduce the Biro in the United States and effectively wage a legal attack against Reynolds's "patent infringement," the Rocket became an instant (and short-lived) phenomenon, selling in thousands of stores and amassing $5.7 million in sales. Staging various stunts to promote his pen, Reynolds unflinchingly boasted that the Rocket was smear-proof and would write in the most adverse conditions—even under water. He also tried to legally block the Biro/CA's entry into the U.S. market, but Eversharp managed to launch its ballpoint in late 1945.

That much-ballyhooed debut was supposed to bolster Eversharp's stature in the pen world (the company's **Skyline** fountain pen was already a major success). It instead turned out to be a colossal business failure, and the Biro/CA, according to numerous pen experts, soon became known as "the pen that killed Eversharp."

The Rocket also fizzled. Confronted by numerous competing companies that hoped to profit from the ballpoint craze, Reynolds promised that the pen would write for two years without refilling, leaking, or skipping. Once the Rocket failed to live up to the hype, the company was forced to issue refunds and, in a sea of debt, folded in 1951.

But Eversharp took the biggest bath. Failing to win its (expensive) lawsuit against Reynolds, the company hurriedly launched the CA instead of thoroughly testing the ballpoint and ensuring its quality. As *PenHero.com*'s Jim Mamoulides suggests, "High expectations, both from advertising and from Eversharp's reputation as a first-tier pen manufacturer, led to great disappointment from customers, and when coupled with virtually unconditional guarantees, led to disaster for the company. Almost the entire production for the year was returned."

Eversharp made its CA in **Fifth Avenue**, **Skyline**, and **Retractable** models, although the Fifth Avenue was always advertised simply as the Eversharp CA. But none of this helped. Faced with even stiffer competition from less expensive brands, Eversharp started to produce ballpoints for a dollar and even less in the late 1940s. But these unreliable pens, according to Mamoulides, only increased the public's distaste for ballpoints, and in 1957 Eversharp finally bowed to the inevitable. After pouring millions of dollars into failed advertising campaigns, production, and lawsuits, the company sold its pen business to Parker.

"Lifetime" ballpoints never lived up to their promise. They leaked and skipped, and even their limitless guarantees couldn't persuade skeptical consumers to spend a dollar on a pen. Then came Frenchman Baron Bich. Soon crowned as the low-cost "use and toss" king, the publicity-minded Bich in the early 1950s developed a disposable "writes first time, every time" ballpoint that quickly became an American phenomenon. Realizing that consumers wanted a cheap pen that could be thrown away, this bon vivant and America's Cup racer revolutionized writing by obtaining patent rights to the Biro and implementing a manufacturing process that dramatically lowered the price of a ballpoint to twenty-nine cents.

In the wake of the CA and other overhyped ballpoints, Americans could easily have dismissed Bich's **Crystal Bic**. But the baron, a former production manager in an ink factory, didn't just offer a dependable, no-frills pen. He also saw the future. Spending millions of dollars on advertising, Bich sponsored a national TV campaign to promote the pen, a blitz that featured Bics being strapped onto ice skates, shot out of rifles, and mounted on jackhammers.

Parker tried to compete with Bic by offering the **Jotter** in 1954, which was a well-constructed pen with a tungsten carbide ball, and was relatively successful. But the Bic was so dominant that the baron acquired the Waterman Pen Company in 1960 to help his company compete more effectively against Parker. Once again, Bich proved to be the man with the golden touch, forcing Parker back into the fountain pen market, an industry that fell into rapid decline for the next twenty years.

Bic did have to battle against "the world's smoothest writing instrument," a ballpoint with a "Magic Sphere" system called the **Fisher Anti-Gravity Space Pen (AG-7)**. Touted as the pen that would conquer any material, "paper, linens, or textiles," this bullet-shaped creation was the inspired handiwork of Paul Fisher. A visionary who invented the **universal refill** used in most ballpoints, he exploited the marketing potential of the public's fascination with space exploration. Spending more than a million dollars on research, he ultimately developed a ballpoint that would be associated with NASA's "Right Stuff" Apollo missions.

At the heart of this trailblazing technology was a thick thixotropic ink that was forced toward the pen point by nitrogen. (*Thixotropic* means that the ink would gel when static but could be liquefied when shaken.) Because this pressurized semi-solid did not rely on gravitational forces, the AG-7 was eventually tested by NASA to determine if it would write under such extreme conditions as +150° Centigrade and -120° Centigrade temperatures. The AG-7 performed so admirably that this chrome-plated ballpoint won NASA's imprimatur as "the pen that went to the moon." Now selling for $50, it is still used on all American- and Russian-manned space flights.

Other ballpoints would also make history, or at least have a hand in historical events. Showing his sense of humor, President Harry S. Truman gave Reynolds Rockets to dignitaries at White House gatherings. The pens were printed with the statement "I Swiped This from Harry S. Truman."

As pen collector John Loring notes, several other presidents were pen enthusiasts, as was Winston Churchill, all intent on capturing the moment with a stylized ballpoint. When he was vice president, Richard Nixon alternated between using a blue Reynolds Rocket, a silver metal Parker Jotter, and numerous gold metal ballpoints (of unknown origin) imprinted with his signature. Upon moving into the Oval Office, Nixon favored a **Parker 45** roller ball (or ballpoint), and a **Scripto 200** felt tip. Loring does not mention which pen was used to pardon Nixon, but he suggests that Gerald Ford was also particularly attuned to a pen's finer points.

"Vice President Ford's Parker 45 bill signer had a silver metal cap and trim and a blue plastic barrel imprinted in silver with the Vice Presidential seal and signature," notes Loring. "In addition I know of two 'push-to-activate' ballpoints. One is all gold metal with four smooth rings . . . with his signature on the barrel. The second V.P. Ford ballpoint type has a blue plastic barrel, imprinted with the Vice Presidential seal and signature."

Renowned for his "centrist" positions, President Bill Clinton followed the same middle-of-the-road strategy in choosing pens. He flaunted an elegant-looking Sheaffer fountain pen at bill signings, and was also known to use a **Kwik Kwik** ballpoint (a rare autographed piece Loring sells for $75), and an equally desirable Parker **Insignia** ballpoint (priced at $350).

Most ballpoints sold on the Internet are far less interesting or pricey. The mass-produced ballpoint has mainly become a promotional tool for corporations, hotel chains, and sundry businesses to tout their names, products, and services. Few have any real historical import or the elegant craftsmanship to be called works of art. That lofty distinction belongs to the fountain pen and to the artisans now crafting "retro," individually expressive pens, who, along with paying tribute to the past, are ushering in a new golden age. ▣

7

THE SECOND GOLDEN AGE: 1970–PRESENT

More than a few legends have been reborn and honored in silver, gold, platinum, and diamonds. Fueled by the new collectibles craze (watches, classic cars, vintage toys, and so on), more discretionary income, and a heightened appreciation for Old World–style craftsmanship, a second golden age of pen making is flourishing. A revolt against the impersonality of cyberspace, today's "culture of the hand" renaissance is a throwback to the stylistic ingenuity of Parker and Waterman, a retro design movement that has produced a wealth of meticulously sculptured and jewel-studded limited edition fountain pens.

Whether it's commemoratives of great historical events or tributes to artists and explorers, the parade of mother-of-pearl, gold, and space age fiber pens is

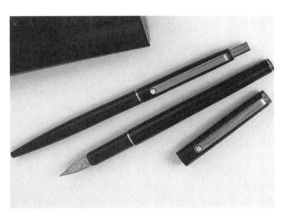

Parker Sonnet
Sterling and
Pelikan 1000,
Late 1990s

Montblanc,
CS Line,
Late 1970s

seemingly endless. With one stroke of the hand, Abraham Lincoln, Charles Lindbergh, and Marilyn Monroe are remarkably resurrected. Houdini lives to stage another magical escape, and Marco Polo's trip to China's Great Wall is rendered in bewitching detail. Equally suggestive of wonders from the Far East, the all-powerful White Tiger of Asia is exquisitely trumpeted as a supernatural figure; while, evocative of their own mesmerizing genius, Ernest Hemingway, Oscar Wilde, and Edgar Allan Poe are fittingly celebrated in handheld works of art.

Certainly a world away from a Bic, Krone has innovatively paid homage to space travel with the **Apollo 11** pen featuring an "embedded" piece of the actual Kapton foil that survived the reentry. Honoring another sort of scientific trailblazer, Delta has recently offered the **Isaac Newton**, a diamond-and-platinum extravaganza limited to only eighty-five pieces. Appreciating heroes of every stripe, this Italian company has feted **Julius Caesar** in a pearled resin pen with hand-engraved horse chariots, totally encrusted its **Napoleon Bonaparte** in a sheath of 18k gold, and beautifully decorated both its **Native American** piece and its salute to filmmaker **Federico Fellini**.

Celebrating other types of monumental figures, Montblanc weighs in with its **Writer's Series**, an assortment of pieces dedicated to such literary stalwarts as Marcel Proust, Agatha Christie, and Fyodor Dostoyevsky.

Japanese pen maker Namiki, famous for its seventh-century-inspired *maki-e* lacquering, vibrantly colored barrels, and unique decorative touches like inlaid abalone shell, combines heroic themes with pure fantasies. Typically juxtaposing powdered gold accents with the shadowiness of black lacquer, this workshop, which is obsessive about quality, is best known for the enameled **Lovebirds** and **Goldfish** from the Yukari Collection. But they are winning new acclaim from the limited edition **Seahorse**, which uses the *raden* lacquering technique of applying mother-of-pearl, as well as the **Hiten**, which features a *suien* or "water flame" cloud of mist atop the sacred East Pagoda of *Yakushi-ji*.

Then there's Omas, an Italian pen maker dating back to 1925. This statement-making Bolognese pioneer, which was one of the first brands to develop celluloid, has traditionally been linked to big concepts. It has crafted pens that honor **Goya**, **Lech Walesa**, and **Galileo**; paid tribute to Buddhism with the **Triratna**, which is covered with 120 grams of gold; crafted the reverential four-pen **Nelson Mandela 80** collection, and styled the **Merveille du Monde**, a hand-wrought gold and jade treasure embellished with *repoussé* representations of the Great Wall, Marco Polo, and Venetian buildings. Omas also designed an ergonomically correct pen exclusively for the Museum of Modern Art, called the **MoMA360**. Its geometric design is accented by three rhodium gold rings. Obviously a lover of

Cross 150th
Anniversary
Limited
Edition 1996

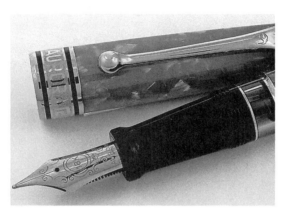

Aurora
Primavera
Limited
Edition 1998

things Italian, Omas's most recent triumph is the delicately painted **Giacomo Casanova** (73 pieces in gold, 725 in silver), a porcelain and gold tribute to the legendary Venetian lover, musician, spy, swordsman, gambler, and adventurer. This radiant pen features a seductive cameo of this provocative figure, a piston-button filling system, and an 18k gold nib ornamented with an irreverent-looking Cupid. At $4,700, the pen, like its namesake, is deliciously wicked.

All this artistic activity indicates a return to the passion and style of the Parker Snake era. Pen magic is back. Yet because this rekindled interest in handcrafted, gold and marbleized writing instruments has prompted scores of companies to issue limited editions, how does the collector distinguish between investment-worthy pieces and pretty pens with little long-term value?

One approach is to buy only pens with a history and a story, those with a thematic concept that is ongoing, such as Montblanc's Writer's Series, which has generated consistent appeal among collectors. More than just an emotional connection with Hemingway or Proust, these highly valued pens carry the imprimatur of a world-renowned company, meet certain manufacturing standards, and are guaranteed to be of limited quantity. By satisfying such objective criteria, these pens take on a certain cachet, prestige, or pedigree, and, if rare enough, can actually be esteemed as blue chips—the very best kinds of investments.

Entrée into this vaunted pantheon demands much more than fancy leather and velvet packaging, a pavé diamond replica of Seattle's Space Needle, or a new NASCAR-tested carbon fiber. Companies such as Cartier, Namiki, Michel Perchin, Aurora, and Pelikan have won such recognition by styling classics, pens that embody timeless values of elegance, craftsmanship, and smoothness. In a world that is increasingly fast-paced and ephemeral, limited editions celebrate the truly memorable, such as Jerusalem's three-thousand-year history, Voltaire, or the Ming Dynasty, and not some passing fancy or questionable commemorative. Is a summit meeting, pop hero, or Guinness World Record really worthy of a $2,500 pen?

"Now that companies are coming into this market with all sorts of status symbol pens, it's very tough to pick and choose," says Terry Wiederlight, co-owner of New York's Fountain Pen Hospital, the world's largest pen emporium. "Yet after getting past all the hype of what's a 'hot' fashion statement, the key to selecting a truly great piece is the name of the manufacturer. Going with established brands, those that have a proven track record for quality and service, is a must."

These investment-worthy limited editions are true storytellers: They bring a subject to life and magically transport collectors to another era. Krone has certainly tried to make its pens historically relevant by embedding a piece of Mt. Everest in the **Sir Edmund Hillary Mountain Everest**, a portion of the *Spirit of St. Louis*'s engine in the **Charles Lindbergh**, and Abraham Lincoln's DNA into its **Limited Edition Abraham Lincoln** Pen. (Strange as it may sound, Krone claims to have taken "highly authenticated strands of Abraham Lincoln's hair," reproduced the DNA, and embedded it in crystallized form in the amethyst stone of the pens.) But other companies have also connected with the past to style memorable works of art.

Based in Florence, Italy, Visconti relives the glory of dynastic China with its **Happiness** or **Fortune Dragon** limited edition, a red and black ebonite piece with gold accents that celebrates Beijing's Temple of Heaven.

Urushi lacquering is the specialty of Nakaya. Painting five types of *Kiku* flowers with gold powder and sprinkling this "long life, no sickness" talisman with flecks of proprietary gold, silver, and blue powder, artisans at this Japanese company have fashioned the **Chrysanthemum**, a work of art that echoes the majesty of the Far East.

Indebted to the fabled Peter Carl Fabergé and his dazzling collection of bejeweled eggs and figurines, Michel Perchin is noted for his **Blue, Red, Green, and Gold Ribbed** line of *guilloched* translucent enamel pens. *Guilloche* is an engraved pattern applied to metal to give it a waved look. The company's **Red and Gold Monogram** is crafted from .925 sterling silver and twenty-three layers of enamel, and plated with 22k yellow gold; its stunning high-relief design reaches new heights of beauty.

Aurora's 80th Anniversary Pen has a sterling silver body and cap with *guilloche* flame decorations. David Oscarson's **Crystal Collection** features a handblown, cut, and polished "Reed and Pellet" design. The Italian pen maker Montegrappa offers the **Oriental Zodiac** line of luxury pieces covered in gold and silver, featuring designs inspired by the signs of the dragon, rabbit, horse, and so on.

Limited Edition Buyer's Guide

Whatever your tastes, these are key points to remember when purchasing limited edition pens:

- Avoid commemoratives of questionable historical importance.
- Regularly visit the web sites of the major pen makers to be aware of their new offerings.
- Preserve the packaging and documentation that accompany limited editions. These papers add to the pen's value.
- Mint condition limited editions are more valuable than those that have been used.
- Don't be fooled by gold nibs. Almost all contemporary limited editions feature a gold nib.
- Scarcer pens are usually a better investment than pieces that have been produced in larger numbers.
- Purchase pens only from long-established or "brand equity" companies.
- Avoid "once in a lifetime" specials on the Internet.
- To derive more enjoyment from a limited edition, familiarize yourself with the history or background of that particular pen.

Price List: 1970–2000s

Because of the rich and diverse array of fountain pen models, the collector is confronted by a wide number of ink-fill systems and decorative features. It is therefore crucial to understand the abbreviations that are used on web sites and in retailers' catalogs:

- **GD**   Good Condition
- **GF**   Gold Filled
- **GP**   Gold Plated
- **K**   Karat
- **LF**   Lever Filler
- **PF**   Piston Filler
- **STSL**   Sterling Silver
- **VT**   Vermeil Trim

The following price guide lists a sampling of limited edition pens produced during pens' second golden age. Brief pen descriptions are included, along with the abbreviated names of reputable, well-established retailers who have at one point sold a particular pen (see "Pen Pals" in the Resource Guide for contact information). It must be noted that prices fluctuate, and it is best to contact the dealers for current market values.

- **DN**   David Nishimura Vintage Pens
- **EB**   eBay
- **FPH**   Fountain Pen Hospital
- **GP**   GoPens
- **PB**   PenBox
- **PEN**   Penopoly
- **PH**   PenHome

Aurora
Saint Petersburg, 2003, pink or blue finish,
150 fountain pens produced, PF $1,200, FPH

Aurora
88 Demonstrator, GP trims, 1,888 produced,
18k nib $339, EB

Aurora
Leonardo da Vinci, 2002, lacquer/gold plate,
499 fountain pens produced $1,095, FPH

Aurora
Giuseppe Verdi/Gran Gala, 1999 $1,500, FPH

Caran D'Ache
La Gotica, 2003, 1,140 produced $3,600, FPH

Cartier
Art deco, silver-plated, 2003 $1,060, FPH

Cartier
Must de Cartier, 1985, converter, France,
Godron design in silver plate with red inlaid
clip, 18k nib, exc $240, PH

Conklin
100th Anniversary crescent filler, 2001,
STSL/celluloid, 388 produced $1,200, FPH

Delta
Indigenous People–Native American, 2003,
VT, LF, 1,492 produced, LF $695, FPH

Delta
20th Anniversary, 2002, VT, 982 produced,
LF, vermeil $560, FPH

Delta
Napoleon Bonaparte, 2002, sterling/blue
edition, 808 produced $1,150, FPH

Delta
Republic of the Seas, Mediterranean blue,
cartridge/converter filler, rhodium plated, original
box, 18k nib $369, EB

Delta
Julius Caesar, red/STSL $750, FPH

Delta
Nazareth, 2000, solid
gold trim $2,300, ($850 regular red, no gold), FPH

Krone
Marilyn Monroe, 2003, ivory celluloid and
gold edition, 288 produced $5,500, FPH

Krone
Python, 2003, hand-painted python skin,
80 produced $2,750, FPH

Krone
General George Patton, 2003, olive green
and sterling, four stars on the cap,
288 produced $3,750, assorted sources

Krone
Michelangelo, 2002, carved ivory,
188 produced $5,900, FPH

Krone
Moses, 2003, 288 produced $3,500, assorted sources

Krone
Babe Ruth, 288 produced $2,800, FPH

Krone
Abraham Lincoln, 1998, 1,008
produced $1,650, assorted sources

Krone
William Shakespeare, 1999, .950 platinum,
STSL, and white 18k, 388 produced $3,400, FPH

Krone
Apollo 11, .925 STSL accents, 488 produced $2,500, FPH

Marlen
20th Anniversary, 2003, Diamond edition,
20 pens produced $14,500, FPH (Marlen also makes
                        a limited edition with silver trim at
                        $5,500, and in solid rose gold at
                        $40,000), call for availability, FPH

Marlen
*Cadran Solaire Sundial, STSL edition,
138 produced worldwide* $5,500, FPH

Marlen
*Coral Incantation Jewel Cameo, 2003, coral/
sterling/solid gold, 81 produced*   call for availability, FPH

Michel Perchin
*The Cuckoo, .925 STSL, fashioned after
Imperial Russian Fabergé egg, opaque black
enameling, 18k nib* $4,290, EB

Michel Perchin
*Amber art deco, .925 STSL barrel, engraved,
guilloche, cap crown and clip finished in
22k gold vermeil, enameled in amber,
cabochon tiger eye* $3,000, EB

Montblanc
*Carrera Triple Set, 1972, fountain pen, injector
pencil, 4-color ballpoint, yellow and black,
pencil barrel sound but has three hairlines
next to cone and cap, fountain pen uses
cartridges, fine-plus* $205, DN

Montblanc
*12 Masterpiece, 1970, PF, black 12 with slip
cap, ink view window, exc* $240, PH

Montblanc
*Qing Dynasty, 88 produced, cap made of jade,
with dragon in 18k gold, and yellow
diamonds, exc* $8,800, EB

Montblanc
F. Scott Fitzgerald, 15,000 produced $650, FPH

Montblanc
*225 BF, 1971, black matte with brushed GF
cap, mint* $125, GP

Montblanc
Jules Verne, blue lacquer $675, FPH

Montblanc
*Charles Dickens, 2001, 18,000
produced* $750 range on Internet

Montblanc
Charlemagne, 2000, 4,810 produced $2,100, FPH

Montblanc
*402 MonteRosa, 1970, PF, black, steel cap,
ink view windows, exc* $217, PH

Montblanc
Alexandre Dumas, 1996, 15,000 produced $425, EB

Montblanc
Lorenzo de Medici, 1992,
4,810 produced   *$4,500 to $5,000, FPH*

Montblanc
149 Meisterstück or Masterpiece,
1995, black, gd   *$285, PH*

Montblanc
Solitaire Doué, piston converter, black/gold-plated,
18k nib inlaid with platinum, barrel/cap
gold-plated   *$350, EB*

Montblanc
Hemingway, 1992, mint, 25,000 produced   *$2,500, FPH*

Montegrappa
White Nights, 2003, STSL, 1,305 produced,
solid gold with precious stones
        $21,550, ($2,490 for standard edition), FPH

Montegrappa
Journey on the River Rhine, 2003, STSL,
500 produced   *$970, FPH*

Montegrappa
Russia Cosmopolitan   *$970, FPH*

Montegrappa
Amerigo Vespucci, 2002, STSL/celluloid   *$2,500, FPH*

Montegrappa
Human Civilization, 2001, sterling/enamel,
1,912 produced   *$2,350, FPH*

Montegrappa
Tertio Millennium, 1998, 1,912 produced   *$2,100, FPH*

Montegrappa
Millennium Dragon, 2000, yellow resin/STSL,
366 produced   *$1,450, FPH*

Namiki
Seahorse, 2003, abalone inlay, cartridge
converter, 300 produced   *$1,900, FPH*

Namiki
Maki-e design, 1970, converter   *$2,900, PH*

Namiki
Pilot 85th Anniversary, maki-e lacquering/STSL,
75 pens available in the U.S., cartridge
converter   *$1,900, Internet*

Namiki
King Cobra, 2001, maki-e,
700 produced   *$1,600, Internet*

Namiki
Yukari Pigeon and Persimmon,
maki-e lacquering   *$2,700, Internet*

Omas
Giacomo Casanova, 2003, enamel and silver
vermeil, 725 produced $1,595 silver, $4,695 gold, FPH

Omas
Venice Carnevale, 2003, black and white
lacquer, PF, 1,458 produced $850, FPH

Omas
Mandela/Birth of Royalty, 1999, STSL,
1,600 produced $1,600, FPH

Omas
Mandela/The Struggle, 1999, STSL,
1,600 produced $1,600, FPH

Omas
Mandela/Africa, 1999, STSL,
1,600 produced $1,600, FPH

Omas
Hong Kong, 1997, STSL, 1,997 produced
                    $1,800 silver, $10,000 gold, FPH

Omas
Jerusalem, 1996, STSL, 3,000 produced
                    $1,600 silver, $8,000 gold, FPH

Omas
Marconi, 350 produced, celebrates 100th anniversary of
radio, PF, 18k nib, originally $3,800 $800, EB

Omas
Galileo Galilei, working condition, 18k
two-tone nib $549, EB

Omas
Artaxan PF, 1985, bright red PF, GF trim   €190, PH

Parker
75 Bicentennial Americana, 1976, LF, mint,
in box $800, PEN

Parker
Duofold Centennial, 1992, Converter filler, marbled
maroon, original box/papers $900, PH

Parker
Duofold Centennial, 1994, GP, long clip
with raised feathers, box/papers $495, PH

Parker
Mandarin Yellow Duofold, 1995, 10,000
produced, mint box/papers $695, PH

Parker
75, 1980, converter, Prince de Galles broad
band design, good $135, PH

Parker
Snake, 1997, replica of original eyedropper issued
in 1900s, 5,000 produced in silver, 250 in gold,
snake overlay in silver $2,500, FPH

Parker
61 Presidential, 1974, converter, 9k fine barley,
original leatherette box $945, PH

Parker
45 Flighter, 1982, stainless steel cap and body,
made in England, uses cartridge or converter
filler, nm $85, DN

Parker
75 Milleraies, 1983, fine parallel lines pattern in
silver plate, made in France, includes converter,
mint $205, DN

Parker
61, 1972, rage red AF, frosty Lustraloy cap, perfect
sac transparency, mint $275, DN

Parker
75, 1970s, 100 percent STSL checked pattern,
converter filler or ink cartridge, 14k nib, AF $165, JG

Parker
45 Harlequin set in box, 1981, circlet pattern
fountain pen and ballpoint, stainless steel
cap and barrel, made in England, box has
broken hinge, mint $205, DN

Parker
Premier, 1983, converter, unused, in Chinese
lacquered finish, exc-nm $318, PH

Pelikan
M200 Demonstrator, 1996, green transparent,
black turning knob $200, GP

Pelikan
Myth of the Moon Goddess, 2003, Toledo finish,
sleeve of .925 silver with 24k gold overlay,
568 produced $2,350, FPH

Pelikan
M200 Demonstrator, 2001, transparent piston
filler, 12.5 cm long, GP trim, mint $150, DN

Pelikan
1935, green celluloid, 4,000 produced $900, FPH

Sheaffer
Mount Everest, 2,003 produced $600, FPH

Sheaffer
Balance, 1999, converter, jade green, mint $190, PH

Sheaffer
Balance, 1999, converter, unused "amber glow,"
18k two-tone feather-touch nib $217, PH

Stipula
Pinocchio, 2003, red/black ebonite,
piston fill, 881 produced $680, FPH; $300, EB

Stipula
Etruria 10th Anniversary, 2001,
celluloid/sterling, 991 produced $550, FPH

Stipula
Il Dono, STSL, 988 produced $2,500, FPH

Visconti
Divine Comedy Vermeil Fountain Pen,
2002, cream celluloid/scrimshaw,
388 produced $1,500, EB

Visconti
Fortune Dragon, 2001, ebonite and vermeil,
888 produced $890, FPH

Visconti
Taj Mahal, rose gold/vermeil filigree, 1996,
388 produced $2,470, FPH

Waterman
Edson White Limited, 2003, STSL,
4,000 produced $1,000, FPH

Waterman
Opera FB, 1987, converter, black guilloche
finish, exc $556, PH

■

8

THE INSTANT
EXPERT QUIZ

1. What are the rarest and most prized pens?

2. Why is the Parker Snake so coveted?

3. What is the most prized limited edition?

4. What distinguishes Namiki from other brands?

5. Which ballpoint pens have the best resale value?

6. What pens should be avoided?

7. Which is a more desirable category, vintage or contemporary limited editions?

8. When do vintage pens need to be reconditioned?

9. Should vintage fountain pens be used or only displayed?

10. How is a pen's value determined?

11. What's the best way to buy pens?

12. If a pen has cracks, should it be avoided?

13. What pens are most prone to fakes and forgeries?

14. How can you spot a counterfeit pen?

15. What is meant by a pen's "condition"? What should a collector be sure to look for?

16. How are fountain pens cleaned and how often should this be done?

17. How can leaks be prevented?

18. What are the best ways to store pens?

19. Which lesser-known pen manufacturers are likely to increase in value in the future?

20. Should collecting pens be mainly a fun-filled hobby or an investment?

Answers

1. This is a matter of considerable debate, but many experts will opt for Parker **Aztecs**, **Giraffes**, **Giants**, and **Snakes**. Other aficionados will choose early Waterman pieces such as the $5,500 **Doll's Pen**, one of the company's **Swastikas**, an eyedropper from the early 1900s, or a **Safety** pen. In any case, these highly pursued and rare pieces from the past are investment-quality works of art.

2. Although the snake is an ancient symbol of evil and betrayal, this legendary Parker pen is the ultimate representation of the pen maker's art. Adorned with emeralds and either a sterling silver overlay or two gold reptiles wrapped around the body of the pen, this 1906 *repoussé* treasure was hand-designed by Heath, an esteemed jewelry maker of that era. Typically igniting heated competition at auctions, this $30,000 piece is arguably the most beautiful pen ever crafted.

3. There is no one pen that is the most prized. Yet several pieces have generated tremendous allure over the past ten years, and continue to appreciate in value every year. Montblanc's **Lorenzo de Medici** and **Hemingway** pens are true blue chip assets, Aurora's **Benvenuto Cellini,** originally priced at $8,500 with a solid gold overlay, was produced in very small quantities to

solidify its investment value, and both the Omas **Hong Kong** or **Return to the Motherland** and the **Jerusalem 3000** (with *repoussé* scenes from the Holy City) continue to rise in value—and even more important, to stir the fascination of well-heeled collectors.

4. This Japanese company crafts exquisite pens heralded for their *maki-e*, or hand-lacquering technique, that dates back to the seventh century. Pens from Namiki's Emperor's Collection use black lacquer, inlaid abalone shell, burnished charcoal, and gold flecks in a symphony of flawless craftsmanship. These pens are innovative and wondrously detailed.

5. Ballpoints such as 1960s' **Fisher Space Pens** and Reynolds's **Rockets** from the 1940s are difficult to find yet continue to attract collector interest. Eversharp **CA**s also attract attention. Ballpoints and roller balls that accompany name-brand fountain pens (or original sets) have a steady following. Ballpoints that are "gimmicky" are another collectible, such as the Colibri **Mickey Mouse Scribe** (there's also a **Goofy** model), which is actually a three-way pen: a fountain pen, roller ball, and ballpoint. Beginners looking for low-cost ballpoints will be intrigued by the **Jac Zagoory Collection** of stainless ballpoints and the **Messograf Ball Point** and **Callipers** model.

6. Those that are billed on the Internet as a "once in a lifetime" offering. Also beware of relatively unknown brands or pens with gold-wash plating. These are not bargain pens. They are just filler for the garbage dump.

7. Vintage pens require more attention than contemporary pens. Early eyedropper-fill pens can be cumbersome and messy, and many vintage pieces are extremely delicate. Yet vintage pens that were built with sturdy materials are often more expertly designed than modern pens. The allure and rarity—plus the historical value—of many antique pens also makes them, according to many experts, better investments than newly issued limited editions that have a much shorter track record as investments. The market in limited editions, as many retailers complain, is just

becoming too crowded, and that has cheapened the value of many contemporary pens.

8. David Nishimura, an expert on pen restoration, thinks that pens with rubber sacs should be reconditioned every ten years. As he explains, "Certain inks seem to be harder on sacs than others, and there are also significant variables such as temperature, humidity, and level of pollutants."

9. A pen in mint condition will definitely retain its value, if untouched. Yet using a pen is also fun, a mark of discernment and sophistication that separates the user from the crowd. Many collectors settle this conundrum by keeping one supply of vintage pens that are to be used, while other, perhaps more delicate pens are strictly kept in pristine condition.

10. Read company histories, go to pen web sites, talk with other collectors, and visit pen shows to determine which pens are valuable. There are no professional grading services such as in the collectible coin market to give pens a definite imprimatur of rarity. Research and self-education are the only ways to determine which pens are most coveted.

11. At pen shows where the buyer profits from the keen competition between exhibitors or sellers, and where pens can be tested to see if they write well, or are otherwise in accordance with the personal tastes of the buyer.

12. Not necessarily. David Nishimura says that while cracks were once reason enough to stay away from these pens, "There's been a growing acceptance of cracks, as long as they are stable and unobtrusive, and preferably well-sealed. This acceptance makes sense, especially when the pen in question is going to be used and where functionality takes precedence over a pristine state of preservation."

13. Like any industry with high-price, high-profile collectibles, many of the most collectible and rare "blue chips" have attracted counterfeiters and scam artists. Those pens with Toledo-work overlays, such as **Waterman** and **Montblanc**, are often copied (albeit slop-

pily). Nishimura also warns collectors to watch out for **Parker 51**s, **Duofold Senior Lucky Curve Deluxes**, and **Pelikans** with metal overlays. Fortunately, most of the counterfeits made over the years were not exact, and often merely replicas, so it can be easy to tell them from the real thing.

14. Since pen collecting has become such a high-priced market, there are lots of fakes to watch out for. The best defense against counterfeit pens is to know the original very well. One of the most common problems with fakes is very poor fit and finish—parts don't fit together tightly, seams show, edges aren't finished, paint or plating is not full coverage. Also watch out for rough engravings, as expected when copied, rather than smooth artistry as from the original machining. Nibs may be marked gold but are actually gold-plated steel. Some of these nibs will be magnetic, and therefore obvious fakes. Others will need a destructive scratch test to see if the plating will come off. Really bad fakes will use wrong materials: plastic Montblancs made of metal or in finishes Montblanc never offered, or generic "Iridium Tip Germany" nibs on brand name pens.

15. Because there are no professional grading services for pens, there are no universal standards to describe a pen's condition. Every retailer will select his or her own definitions of excellent, good, near mint, or fine. New collectors should make their own examinations, carefully evaluating whether a pen shows noticeable signs of wear, whether it is fully functional, whether the manufacturer's imprints are clearly discernible, and the extent of brassing (when the plating wears off to reveal brass base metal) to the trim. Most typically, *mint* means unused, *near mint* indicates that the pen has been used yet shows no signs of wear, *excellent* denotes minimal wear, and *very good* defines a pen that shows definite signs of wear but few dings or scratches. Original boxes or cases, accompanied by original documentation, can add to a pen's attractiveness and value, but these trappings are of secondary importance to the pen's overall appearance and functionality.

16. Most experts agree that pens should be cleaned every three months. Clean the nib, barrel, and cap with cold water under a faucet, or let it soak for a half hour in a shallow bowl of water. Dry the nib, barrel, and cap with a paper towel, then repeat the process. Periodic cleaning will make sure that there is no dried ink in the pen, which can block the ink-feed system.

17. Always keep pens filled, and carry them with the nib pointed upward. Jim Gaston also recommends that you "dry the nib and cap with a lint- and oil-free cloth only."

18. Keep pens away from direct sunlight in a cool, dry place. Because resins in vintage pens interact with each other, you should try to keep pens separated in pouches or display cases. Don't use cases with foam rubber, because that could cause discoloration. Leather cases should be lined to prevent scratching or denting, and avoid leather cases using preservatives. These preservatives in the leather can tarnish or damage plated metal parts and blacken sterling silver. Generally avoid leather cases unless they are known to be "pen friendly." Plastic cases don't always shield pens from heat or sunlight. Choose a case wisely. Pen stores and web sites offer many kinds, from simple to deluxe.

19. **Aiken Lambert** and pens from **John W. Carter**. The experts also expect many **Sheaffers** to rise in value and importance, as well as **Conklins** and **Conway Stewarts**.

20. Many rare **Parkers** and **Watermans** continue to appreciate in value, to unprecedented and stunning levels. But, first and foremost, a pen is a writing instrument, meant to be enjoyed for its craftsmanship and distinctive styling. Pens are historical artifacts that evoke a world before computers, when writing a letter could take an entire day. Collecting vintage pens is an exciting and thought-provoking hobby—a joy offering far more important pleasures than mere profits and balance sheets. ◼

RESOURCE GUIDE

PEN PALS: CLUBS, SOCIETIES, ORGANIZATIONS

The Accademia Italiana Penna Stilografica

Since the 1920s Italian companies have crafted exquisite pens with fancy overlays in precious metals, or with laminated celluloid pieces, and that glorious history is celebrated by this club. Along with sponsoring conventions and a newsletter, the Accademia *helps members identify Italian brands that stand at the pinnacle of their craft. Further information is available at* http://xoomer.virgilio.it/leia copi/index.html, *or by e-mail at* jacopini@gr.tdnet.it.

The Baltimore Fountain Pen Society

This group offers convivial friendship, along with the sharing of pen stories, show and tell, and paper and inks to sample at club meetings. It is a haven for pen lovers. For more information, e-mail terlur@jhmi.edu.

The International Fountain Pen Club Armando Simoni

Named after the founder of the legendary Omas brand (that still artfully styles stunning pens), this society awards new members with a lustrous twelve-faceted orange pen. The club regularly sends out newsletters, and will send out back issues (upon request) of its formerly published magazine, which featured articles from experts about pens and pen collecting. Omas is fabled for its wondrous creations, and joining this club, based in Bologna, Italy (€185 or $230), will be a link to a rich cultural tradition. For more information go to www.comune.bologna.it/iperbole/clu bisas/indexuk.htm *or e-mail* clubisas@iperbole.bologna.it.

Pen Collectors of America (PCA)

The publishers of the informative Pennant *journal, this camaraderie-oriented organization is devoted to the admiration, history, and use of vintage pens. For $30 a year members can use the organization's extensive library, trade pens and parts with fellow enthusiasts, and acquire old catalogs, advertisements, and repair manuals. Information about pen shows is also provided. More information about this society can be obtained at* www.pencollectors.com, *by e-mailing* info@pencollectors.com, *or by calling* (319) 372-0881.

Rambling Snail

On a "mission to facilitate research and cultural acceptance of the time-honored art form of the fountain pen," this network offers insightful reviews of pens, a chat room, an encyclopedic array of historical information, and above all, a community of like-minded pen lovers. Visit www.ram blingsnail.net.

The Society of Inkwell Collectors
Dedicated to the proposition that fountain pens feed off of attractive and antique inkwells, this society offers a veritable sponge of information about inkwell esoterica. If pursuing artfully crafted inkwells and sharing this joy with others sounds exciting, the S.O.I.C. and its Stained Finger bulletin can be yours for $35. Find them at www.soic.com, by e-mailing director@soic.com, or by calling (309) 579-3040.

Southeast Pen Collectors' Club
Bring your pens and share with other enthusiasts every Sunday in Smyrna, Georgia. See www.sepencollectors.com or call (770) 434-8677.

Web links to many other pen clubs, shows, manufacturers, and informational sites can be found at *www.Pensations.com* and at any of the other web sites mentioned in this book.

Particular interests can be found through Internet search engines—for example, by keying "fountain pen" + "collectors" into Google, Yahoo, or other search engines.

PENS ON THE INTERNET

1001Pens
If you want to know more about Esterbrook, A. A. Waterman, John Holland, and scores of other pen manufacturers, this retailer provides snapshot histories, plus a comprehensive listing of pen prices (along with pictures of available pens). www.1001pens.com or e-mail service@1001.pens

Arthur Brown International Pen Shop
Showcasing such eminent brands as Omas, Michel Perchin, Krone, and Delta, this long-established New York City retailer is renowned for its vast array of limited editions. www.art brown.com, e-mail penshop@artbrown.com, or telephone (800) 772-PENS

Battersea Pen Company
The sponsors of the London Pen Show repair and stock vintage pens, beauties from Pelikan, Parker, Conway Stewart, Montblanc, and Namiki. The proprietors are experts at refurbishing pens. www.penhome.co.uk, e-mail orders@penhome.co.uk, or telephone 0870-900 1888

Berliner Pen
A fount of information. Avid collector Geoffrey Berliner repairs hard-to-service older pens and is the intelligent

*source for acquiring hard-to-find gems from the past. His
web site provides tips on how to buy vintage pens, as well
as listing those contemporary limited editions that stand
the best chance of appreciating in value.*

*Visit his New York City shop at 928 Broadway, Suite 203, go
to www.berlinerpen.com, e-mail BerlinerPN@aol.com, or
call (800) 440-PENS*

Bill's Pens

*A variety of Parker 51s are available, along with reprints of
vintage company brochures and catalogs, books about
fountain pens, and a guide to pen shows.
www.billspens.com, e-mail Bill@billspens.com, or mail to
Bill Acker, P.O. Box 338, Henderson, TX 75653*

Bittner

*Along with showcasing the David Oscarson Crystal
Collection, provocative Krone limited editions, Visconti, and
other masterful pens, this Carmel, California, retailer offers
a fine line of cotton-laid, archival, embossed, and linen stationery. www.bittner.com, e-mail info@bittner.com, or telephone (888) BITTNER*

Classic Fountain Pens

*Besides offering a wonderful selection of Namiki, Omas,
and Pelikan treasures, this site is the address for repairing,
modifying, and customizing nibs. Whether it's re-tipping,
straightening, or repairing a crack, nib master John
Mottishaw, who stocks arguably the world's largest collection of hard-to-find nibs, will enhance your writing experi-
ence with a more efficient and attractive nib.
www.nibs.com, e-mail John@nibs.com, or telephone
(323) 655-2641*

Fountain Pen Hospital

*Collector Bill Cosby's favorite address for finding limited edi-
tions and vintage pens, this treasure trove offers hard-to-find
Wahl-Eversharp Gold Seals, Parkers with gold-filled filigree,
prized Montblancs, and Conway Stewarts (all beautifully
pictured), as well as excellent repair service and the world's
largest inventory of contemporary pens. www.fountainpen
hospital.com, e-mail info@fountainpenhospital.com, or
telephone (800) 253-7367 and (212) 964-0580*

Fountain Pen Resources/Bruce Marshall

*See striking photos of Parkers, Conklins, Moores, and
Swans, as well as a comprehensive list of pen repair people,
retailers, ink specialists, and much, much more at one of
pendom's most appealing sites. www.brucemarshall.org or
e-mail k1aj@bellatlantic.net*

Fountain Pen Restoration Services

*Offering highly specialized restoration of caps, gold bands,
and clips, this site displays before and after photos of Daniel
Kirchheimer's works.*

http://home.comcast.net/~kirchh/Pen_Restoration *or e-mail* kirchh@trilon.com

Glenn's Pen Page

Offering a definitive listing of great pen shops in various parts of the world, tips on visiting the Waterman factory, and reviews of fine pens, this page speaks to passionate aficionados and budding collectors.
www.marcuslink.com/pens *or e-mail* info@marcuslink.com

Golden Quill

A distinctive range of sealing waxes, pens, inkwells, and an assortment of elegant stationery. www.thegoldenquill.com *or e-mail* thegoldenquill@hotmail.com

GoPens

Comprehensive price catalogs with hundreds of vintage pens are offered at this site, along with full condition reports and reliable pricing information. Photos of pens are provided, and collectors will find it hard to resist purchasing these beautifully displayed vintage pieces. Internationally known dealer and pen collector Gary Lehrer also does appraisals and publishes Quarterly Illustrated Vintage Pan Collecting. www.gopens.com, *e-mail* garylehrer@aol.com, *or telephone (203) 389-5295*

Ink Blotters

Colorful blotters on vintage papers, artfully illustrated with the names of pen manufacturers and other images, such as the 1928 Duofold Monoplane, or Parker 51 Beechcraft. www.inkblotters.com, *e-mail* provisorpro@earthlink.net, *or telephone (847) 566-3400*

Ink Flow

Hundreds of appealing limited editions and more moderately priced collections, inks, and accessories. www.theinkflow.com *or e-mail* finepens@theinkflow.com

Ink Palette

Pens deserve adoring treatment, and this company provides a vast selection of special inks that perfectly complement fine writing instruments. www.inkpalette.com, *e-mail* inkdrop@iglou.com, *or telephone (888) 311-1025*

Jerry Burton's Paper and Pens

Reasonably priced Esterbrooks, Eversharps, Sheaffers, and Parkers are handsomely displayed along with information on prices and condition. Jerry also sells vintage postcards, autographs, lighters, and watches. www.consolidatedmarkets.com, *e-mail* Jerry@consolidatedmarkets.com, *or telephone (253) 581-2494*

Jim Griffiths

Avid pen collector and retailer provides information and pricing about hard-to-find Montblancs, Pelikans, and other

investment-worthy brands. http://jim.griffiths.home.com cast.net *or e-mail* gryff@aol.com

Jim's Pen Site
This A-to-Z site lists the dates of pen shows, provides numerous collecting tips, features hundreds of photos of Jim Gaston's personal favorites, reprint articles by pen experts, and also shares pen folklore. Shop here for antique catalogs, salesmen's pen cases, and other ephemera. www.jimgas ton.com *or e-mail* jim@jimgaston.com

Joon
A purveyor of the world's finest contemporary pens. www.joon.com, *e-mail* pens@joon.com, *or telephone* (800) 782-JOON

Nakaya Fountain Pen
Welcome to the bewitching world of gorgeous green pine needle celluloid pens, maki-e *or* urushi *lacquer pieces, the Celestial Maiden's Robe of Feathers pen, and the* kiku zukushi *series of flowered enticements. Beautifully illustrated, this site celebrates exquisite craftsmanship and awe-inspiring Japanese classics.* www.nakaya.org/eindex.html *or e-mail* nakaya@platinum-pen.co.jp

Nathan Tardif's Vintage Pens and Repair
When emergency surgery is needed, Nat performs his magic, repairing cracked nibs, restoring plunger fillers, and stemming leaks. E-mail him at repairpens@aol.com

Paper Trail Antiques
Lots of interesting inkwells for sale, and pictures of these timeless collectibles. www.papertrailantiques.com

Parker 75
Everything there is to know about the Parker 75, the sterling silver delight with a crosshatch grid pattern that celebrates Parker's 75th anniversary in 1963, along with a few buying tips on how to avoid the author's "hall of shame." www.parker75.com

Penbox
Conway Stewarts, Mabie Todds, Parker 51s, Montblancs, and other pens are offered by this British retailer and re-

pairer, along with pricing information that can serve as a valuable pricing guide. www.penbox.co.uk, *e-mail* sales@penbox.co.uk, *or telephone* 01302 880860

Pendemonium
Along with offering vintage inks, bottles, stationery, and inkstands, this site combines retailing with historical tidbits, and spotlights pens' fine points with an array of vintage photos. Offering a very comprehensive pricing guide, along with photos of thousands of pens in their online catalogs,

this is an indispensable link. www.pendemonium.com,
e-mail sam@pendemonium.com, *or telephone* (888) 372-
2050

PenHero

*At this storehouse of information there are 228 links to pen
dealers, 211 links to pen manufacturers, and 146 links to
auction houses. Clearly one of pen collecting's most illumi-
nating treasure troves, this repository also offers a wealth of
attractively priced vintage pens and a wide array of
Eversharps, Watermans, Esterbrooks, and other special
pieces from the 1930s and 1940s.* www.penhero.com *or
e-mail* penhero@hotmail.com

Pen Lovers

*This excellent site features an events calendar listing pen
shows across the country, a very thorough index of important pen terms, message boards, a full-color gallery of pen
collections, and links to pen manufacturers and places to
have your pens repaired and restored.* www.penlovers.com,
e-mail info@penlovers.net, *or telephone* (908) 291-1153

Penna

*From lavishly illustrated pictorials and a rundown on shows
and auctions to reviews of the latest products and features
on collecting, this elegant Italian magazine is an extremely
useful tool for collectors.* www.pennamagazine.com *or e-
mail* fdonati@ops.it

Penoply

*Rick Conner, a self-proclaimed "pen fanatic" runs this must-
visit, superbly illustrated web site. Along with tracing the
history and evolution of the fountain pen, this site offers
detailed information about leading pen manufacturers and
their most enthralling creations, and how to correctly fill
pens with the proper inks. Penoply also lists the dos and
don'ts of preserving pens and provides a collection of magazine ads that once glorified Parker and Sheaffer pens.*
www.rickconner.net/penoply *or e-mail* rconner@io.com

Penopoly

*Roger Cromwell calls himself "the biggest pen collector in
the country." He has amassed 5,000 vintage pens that are
for sale on his striking web site, which boasts streaming
video, a chat room, a different repair tip every day, and
maintenance advice. Also available is a CD spotlighting
repair tips for beginners.* www.penopoly.com, *e-mail*
roger@penopoly.com, *or telephone* (510) 886-9284

Pens 101

*How to avoid getting fleeced when buying vintage pens,
what pens to buy when starting off as a collector, and other
general information about pens.* http://members.aol.com/
cfrizzle/home *or e-mail* cfrizzle@aol.com

Penstop Online

Parcels of quill pens, rare Conklins from the 1930s, hand-blown crystal ink bottles, and a gallery of wonderfully photographed limited editions from Omas, Krone, Montegrappa, and Montblanc. Plus handcrafted cherrywood pen storage boxes and various other handsome accessories. www.penstoponline.com *or e-mail* info@penstoponline.com

Pentrace

A rich storehouse of informative articles. Pen lovers examine such subjects as "The Case of the Haunted Pen," "How to Survive a Pen Show," "Vintage Italian Pens," "How to Hot-Rod Your Ballpoint," and "The James Bond Shooting Pen." There are also message boards for finding rarities and "inky linkies" to all the major manufacturers. www.pentrace.com *or e-mail* info@pentrace.com

Pen World

The web site of this popular magazine offers lavish photographs and valuable articles about newly introduced, limited edition, and vintage pens. www.penworld.com, *e-mail* info@penworld.com, *or telephone* (281) 359-4363

Richard Binder Fountain Pens

Take a look at an extensive collection of attractive Conklins, early Watermans, an Eversharp Skyline from the 1940s, and the Parker Duofold Geometric, a.k.a. "the Toothbrush." Then go to informative reference guides and the price list for various repairs and nib servicing. www.richardspens.com *or e-mail* richard@richardspens.com

Santa Fe Pens

Besides providing a place for expert pen restoration services, this site is a source for acquiring vintage pens and a vast array of contemporary pieces. www.santafepens.com

Scribe's Delight

Whether it's exquisite Italian Amalfi paper, handmade papers from European artists, or unusual (and always personally imprintable) stationery, this site makes appealing pen-writing statements. www.scribesdelight.com, *e-mail* info@scribesdelight.com, *or telephone* (800) 866-7367

Southern Scribe

Appraising the value of pens is linked to condition, and this instructive site (its penmeister is a repair expert) details the key criteria that must be considered before purchasing a pen. There are also attractive vintage pens for sale and links to other valuable sites. www.thesouthernscribe.com *or e-mail* penfix@thesouthernscribe.com

Vintage Pen

Along with enticing offerings from the world of collectible watches and classic cars, Jonathan Steinberg's web site relives the history of pens (from an 1819 Scheffer Penographic to a 1930 Conklin Symmetrik and other rarities), provides tips for new collectors, details the worth of various high-quality vintage pens, and further accentuates the beauty of various pieces with colorful images. Don't miss the Parker Ultra-Giant, which holds a baby pen within a larger pen. www.vintagepen.com *or e-mail* info@vintagepen.com

Vintage Pens

Everything from collecting basics and the history of pens to preservation tips and filling instructions. One of the pen world's true experts, David Nishimura sells unusual and classic pens, buys pens, and profiles pieces that have long intrigued collectors. This is an indispensable site for beginners and seasoned collectors, with tips on everything from tools and parts, to selling pens, to how to get started in collecting. www.vintagepens.com, *e-mail* pen.info@vintagepens.com, *or telephone (401) 351-7607*

GLOSSARY

Aerometric
Touted as the "filler of the future" by Parker in 1948 when the 51 pen was introduced, and originally called Foto-fill, this mechanism used a rubber or transparent sac, a metal casing, and a pressure bar. Squeezing the pressure bar made the sac expand, allowing ink to flow into the pen.

Ambering
Darkening in color.

Aztec
A vintage Parker with an Awanyu Indian relief design. Extremely rare and valuable.

Baby
A series of tiny eyedropper and lever-filled pens from the early 1900s. Many were gold or gold filled.

Ballpoint
A ballpoint is a pen with a ball, often with a pitted surface, set in a socket at the end of an ink tube filled with paste-like ink. As the ball rotates, it picks up ink from the ink tube and transfers it to the paper.

Black Giant
Both Red and Black Giants made in the early twentieth century by Parker are very rare hard rubber treasures. The predecessor to the famed Duofold.

Blind Cap
Located at the end of the barrel, this threaded or screw-off piece protects the filling mechanism.

Blood
A very deep red pen with flecks of black that was popularized by Wahl-Eversharp. Rare and pricey.

Blue Diamond
A distinctive mark signifying Parker's lifetime warranty.

Button Filler

A button at the end of the barrel was pressed to activate the internal pressure bar, which in turn squeezed the sac. The resulting vacuum drew ink into the pen.

Brassing

When the plating on a pen wears off to reveal brass base metal

Breather Hole

See Vent Hole

Capillary Filler

This sort of capillary action distinguished the Parker 61 pen. Ink was absorbed by a rolled cellophane reservoir when the pen was dipped into a bottle of ink.

Cartridge Filler

Quick and easy: just inject this cylinder and write. Sheaffer, Parker, and other brands popularized these in the 1950s.

Celluloid

A synthetic plastic made from wood by-products that could be transformed into a wide range of patters and colors. Highly flammable, this material discolors over time. Sheaffer first used celluloid for pens in the early 1920s.

Challenger

A button filler available in a striking array of colors offered by Parker in the 1930s.

Coin Filler

By inserting a coin into a slit on the barrel, the pressure bar inside the barrel was depressed and deflated the sac, which enabled ink to flow into the pen. The 1913-14 Waterman coin filler came with a special coin.

Commando

This plastic Waterman pen was affordably priced for the patriotic Everyman in the 1940s.

Converter

To the delight of fountain pen purists who like the old-fashioned method of dipping a pen into a bottle, these piston filler devices replace cartridges.

Crescent Filler

Featuring a protruding U or crescent-shaped tab to activate the pressure bar and sac, these very collectible pens were a hallmark of Conklin in the 1920s and '30s.

Dip Pens

Predating the fountain pen, these relics lacked an ink-supply mechanism and demanded repeated dunks into an inkwell or a bottle of ink.

Doctor's Pen

Made by Omas, Waterman, and other companies in the 1920s, these elaborate, highly fragile pens featured a compartment for carrying a thermometer.

Duofold

Also known as "Big Red," this hard rubber Parker classic transformed the pen market when it was introduced in 1921, and is arguably the most famous pen ever produced.

Eyedropper Filler

No complicated mechanics or mechanisms. Just unscrew the barrel and squirt ink into the barrel with an eyedropper.

Gold Filled

See Rolled Gold.

Gold Plated

an electroplating process that is a much thinner gold layer than gold filled.

Greek Key

a pattern used on many Wahl pens, which was later adopted by Omas.

Half Overlay

A pen with precious metal covering the barrel but not the cap, as with a full ornamental overlay.

Hard Rubber
Also called ebonite or vulcanite, this was the material of choice until the introduction of plastics in the 1920s.

Hooded Nib
Hoping to add a dash of mystery to their pens, Parker introduced this "jet snout" or conical cone that concealed most of the nib on the immensely popular and often imitated 51 pen in the 1940s.

Hundred Year Pen
A 1940s Waterman that came in an array of striking colors, and offered a 100-year guarantee.

Iridium
A hard metal (with traces of platinum) that is used in high-quality pens because the tip of the nib that actually touches the writing surface must be extremely resistant to wear.

Jewel
A round, ornamental "stone" at the cap top or at the bottom of the barrel. Not a precious gem. Some pens are single jewel, others double jewel.

Lever Filler
The nimble finger approach to pen filling. Flipping a metal lever on the side of the barrel deflates the sac; then after returning the lever to its original position, the pen is ready to be immersed in a bottle of ink. Introduced by Sheaffer in 1912 and widely copied by other companies.

Leverless Filler
Introduced by Mabie Todd Swan, this mechanism relied on an end knob, which, when turned, deflated the sac.

Lucky Curve
Patented in 1894, this Parker invention was supposed to solve the age-old leak problem by using a curved ink-feed tube.

Lustraloy
Matte-finish stainless steel.

Mandarin

Parker's bright yellow Duofold, which was a commercial bust in the 1920s and '30s but is now a prized collectible.

Military Clip

This 1940s wartime clip was placed at the top of the cap so that the pen rested low in the pocket, allowing the pocket flap to be buttoned.

Nozac

A no-sac Conklin 1931 piston filler pen with a herringbone pattern.

Overlay

Gold, sterling silver, or another precious metal decoratively wrapped around the cap or barrel. Vermeil is a gold-plated overlay.

Palladium

White metal alloy that Sheaffer used on its nibs in the 1950s.

Patrician

From 1928 to 1938 Waterman produced this plastic pen with a radiant cap band.

PCA

Pen Collectors of America organization.

Pearl and Black

A mosaic effect with shades of pearl mixed with rich black, featured on celluloid pens in the 1920s and '30s. Apt to discolor.

PFM

Sheaffer's Pen for Men Snorkel filler introduced in 1959. A big, reliable pen now avidly sought by collectors.

Piston Filler

A type of filling mechanism with a knob that is turned to activate a piston, which moves back and forth to fill the pen. Several European makers, such as Pelikan and Montblanc, prefer this mechanism.

Plunger Filler
Sheaffer and Wahl pens from the 1930s used this type of filling mechanism, which has a gasket inside and a rod that must be pumped to fill the pen.

Pressure Bar
A metal mechanism that presses or squeezes against the ink sac to draw ink into the pen.

Repoussé
A floral relief pattern on the barrel, or an ornamental design celebrating a special event or subject. Many of today's higher-priced limited editions feature such handcrafted designs.

Ripple
Various color combinations, such as red and black, rose and yellow, and blue and yellow, used on Waterman pens.

Rolled Gold
Or gold filled. A legal definition where the gold is 1/10th or 1/20th the total content by weight. Rolled gold is a sandwich structure comprised of a base metal, usually brass, silver or nickel silver alloy topped by one or more gold layers. The distinguishing mark, KR, on a pen signifies it is gold filled, not solid gold.

Sac
Latex or rubber ink reservoir used in most fountain pens before the 1960s.

Safety Pen
(or Safeties) So called because they had tight seals that prevented leakage, and they featured retractable nibs. Waterman safeties were immensely popular.

Self-Filler
As opposed to eyedroppers, which were cumbersome and messy to fill, these pens contained an internal filling mechanism and a reservoir of ink.

Signet
A Parker model with gold-filled caps.

Skyline
Lever fillers offered by Wahl-Eversharp in the 1940s.

Sleeve Filler
A rotating or sliding sleeve covering a slot in the barrel, which is operated by the thumb to depress the pressure bar. Used for only a brief time on early Waterman pens, their scarcity makes them a valuable collectible.

Slip Cap
Instead of screwing on to the barrel or being threaded, this cap slid onto the barrel like a slip-on garment.

Snake
Inspired by Aztec and Mayan carvings and serpent gods, this Parker pen with exquisite filigree work, genuine emerald eyes, and a snake wound around the barrel and cap is a collector's showpiece, which can sell from $15,000 to $20,000, depending on the condition.

Snorkel Filler
Introduced by Sheaffer in 1952 and used for about ten years, this elaborate mechanism was equipped with a metal tube extending from a "hidden" feed. This tube was immersed into the ink instead of the nib, so there was no need to wipe away excess ink.

Straight Cap
A cap that is usually the same size as the barrel, and associated with eyedropper pens.

Stub
A blunt-ended nib ideal for calligraphy.

Swastika
The swastika, also known as a Navajo cross, is an ancient good-luck symbol dating back some 3,000 years. The word comes from the Sanskrit svasti, well-being. The symbol has also been used on Parker pens of the same name.

Symetrik
A Conklin pen from the 1930s.

Symphony

Adorned with a metal cap, either chrome or gold, and trimmed with contrasting metal, this Eversharp pen was styled by famed designer Raymond Loewy in 1948.

Taper Cap

Narrowing or coming almost to a point, this style cap was popular in the early 1900s.

Tassie

Held in place by the jewel, this is the ornamental metal ring typically found on Parker 51s.

Touchdown

Launched in 1949, this Sheaffer line of pens used pneumatic air pressure to depress the sac and fill pens.

Triumph

A conical or wrap-around nib pioneered by Sheaffer in 1942, used until 1948, and later the name of a pen.

Twist Filler

Instead of using a pressure bar, this mechanism relies on creating a vacuum after air is released from the sac.

Two-Tone Nib

Gold plus a dash of platinum or rhodium.

Vacumatic

This extremely successful Parker celluloid pen offered two-toned nibs, black jewels, marble patterns, and, with certain models, a large ink capacity. These pump fillers were Parker's signature line from 1933 to 1948. The term also applies to a plunger- or pump-type filler that characterizes the 51.

Vent Hole

An opening in the nib that enables ink to flow through the feed channel. Also called the breather hole.

Visulated

Refers to any part of the pen, usually the barrel or section, that is transparent or windowed so that you can see the ink level inside the pen.

Vulcanite

Hard rubber.

Warranted Nib

Guaranteed to be 14k gold, this nib was made by a nib manufacturer and didn't feature any distinctive markings from the pen company.

Washer Clip

A ring-shaped clip found on Parker Duofolds.

White Dot

A symbol used on Sheaffer's most expensive pens, signifying a lifetime warranty.

Wood Grain

Reddish-orange and black swirls that resemble the patterns found in fine wood.

BIBLIOGRAPHY

BOOKS ABOUT PENS AND COLLECTING

Attwood, David. *The Pen, An Appreciation*. London: Aurum Press, 1998.
Emphasis on pen design.

Clark, Juan Manuel. *Collectible Fountain Pens*. Paris: Flammarion, 2002.
Fact-filled collector's guide to fountain pens past and present, with more than 500 color photographs.

Dragoni, Giorgio, and Giuseppe Fichera. *Fountain Pens: History and Design*. Suffolk: Antique Collectors' Club, 1998.
Historical information about the development of writing and writing instruments, 800 color illustrations.

Erano, Paul. *Fountain Pens Past and Present*. Paducah, KY: Collector Books, 1999.
Full-color photos and black/white advertisement reprints, identification and value guide. Provides overview of the development of the fountain pen along with tips on collecting.

Fischler, George, and Stuart Schneider. *Fountain Pens and Pencils: The Golden Age of Writing Instruments*. Atgen, PA: Schiffer Publishing, 1998.
Also known as the Blue Book. More than 1,000 color plates.

Gostony, Henry, and Stuart Schneider. *The Incredible Ball Point Pen*. Atgen, PA: Schiffer Publishing, 1998.
An extensive history of the ballpoint pen along with patent data.

Jacopini, Letizia. *La Storia della Stilografica in Italia (The History of the Italian Fountain Pen)* (2-volume set). Milan: O.P.S. Editore, 2003.
Bilingual Italian/English, extensive information on Italian pen manufacturers, color photographs throughout.

Jaegers, Raymond G., and Beverly C. Jaegers. *The Write Stuff: A Collector's Guide to Inkwells, Fountain Pens and Desk Accessories.* Iola, WI: Krause Publications, 2000.
A history of ink, ink containers, pen makers, and collecting.

Lambrou, Andreas. *Fountain Pens of the World.* London: Philip Wilson Publishers, 2003.
Extensive information on vintage and modern pens from the United States and abroad, 200 color plates.

Lawrence, Cliff. *Fountain Pens: History, Repair and Current Values.* Paducah, KY: Collector Books, 1977.
Black/white and color, history and development of the fountain pen along with tips on repairing.

Lawrence, Cliff, and Judy Lawrence. *The 1992 Official P.F.C. Pen Guide.* Dunedin, FL: Pen Fancier's Club, 1991.
Black/white and color, fully illustrated, with tips about evaluating pens and judging condition.

Martini, Regina, and Harald Grotowsky. *Pens and Pencils: A Collector's Handbook.* Atgen, PA: Schiffer Publishing, 1997.
Information on filling systems and pen company histories.

Schneider, Stuart, and George Fischler. *Illustrated Guide to Antique Writing Instruments, Revised Edition.* Atgen, PA: Schiffer Publishing, 1997.
Pricing guidelines and pen descriptions.

Steinberg, Jonathan. *Fountain Pens: Their History and Art.* New York: Universe Publishing, 2002.

This book explores such topics as the evolution of the pen, the Great Depression's effect on the pen world, the ballpoint pen, and the rebirth of the pen industry. Includes color photographs.

Traini, Pino. *Stilografiche.* San Paolo: Bolis Edizioni, 1998.

Bilingual Italian/English. A look at Traini's collection, along with photographs of fountain pens and pencils, including photos of rare Sheaffers and Parkers. The author also provides collecting tips.

Tyree, Joel, and Sherell Tyree. *Collecting Fountain Pens: A Primer for Newer Collectors.* Privately published, 2001.

This book, written primarily for novice pen collectors, offers information on selecting pens, shopping for pens (in person and online), and caring for pens.

INDEX